Survival Island

D1502486

Angel On Ice

A Mother's Legacy of
Trusting God's Sovereignty

KIARA S. McCOY

and

CALEB P. McCOY

Cover design: Sarah Collins
Back Cover photo: J Caitlin Ringness
Interior Design: Kristeen Ott

Printed in the United States of America

To 'moments made eternity'

contents

❦

i dwell in the sea. i stand there beside her bed. i think
of where you've led me, i can't admit anything is dead.
you wove the womb, you formed the words. i am full
of fear and wonder, i wait behind and before your work.
hem me back in. make me small. let me heal what is
tearing the seams apart. make me small. hem me back in.
i'll be the last one in this light, with darkness closing in.

there's a feeling in heading home, a kind of comfort
that hurts. it doesn't feel like a choice, when you know
what will occur. i hear sympathy in silencing, i hear
a prayer in your veins, being unwound from
the beginning of whatever we could say. hem me
back in. make me small. let me heal what is tearing
the seams apart. make me small. hem me back in.
i'll be the last one in this light, with darkness closing in.

it's hard to say you know better, but you've always
known best. this is the last time that i'll see you,
in the body that gave me breath. i feel the rage
to fight, for those last seconds of life. i was made
from you, and you from something that will never die.

make me small. hem me back in. i don't want to
let you go, or have to know this is the end.
i have to learn. i need to see. everything is a beginning
born of such severe belief.

—steven paschall and caleb p. mccoy

before the beginning

I am the youngest child and the only boy. I have three older sisters, and I was born on April Fool's day. Yes, you can begin feeling sorry for me. I spent my childhood playing with Barbie dolls and my sisters dressing me in pink tutus. I might have actually liked it. On one very dreadful afternoon while playing on the trampoline, my sisters told me that I wasn't the real Caleb. Rather, I was the alien Caleb and the real Caleb was in a trash bag at the bottom of the pond. They took it one step further by telling me—the alien Caleb—that my alien mother would be coming back any day in her spaceship to take me home. Since that afternoon I have been deathly afraid of any type of blinking light in the night sky. Besides being called an alien child and being forced to play with dolls, I had somewhat of a normal childhood.

I think one of the traits I received from my mother was the ability to express thoughts and feelings in written form. My mom left behind 23 journals and thousands of note cards with Bible verses, quotes, and thoughts—all in her beautiful handwriting. I found this letter about four months ago after cleaning out a closet. She wrote it to my dad on their anniversary three months after I was born:

July 4th, 1981

My dearest,
Happy Anniversary. Our 11th year as a team was one for the
record books. I know we'll look back and laugh. I do believe
the Lord gave us Caleb just for this time of our lives. The
promises He has made are fact, and Caleb reminds us of this
even when there are giants in the way. To God be the glory!

All my love,
Kia

My mom began skating as a seven-year-old in upstate New York and competed until she was in high school when a more rounded lifestyle became appealing to her. She continued to skate several times each week and participated in her club's competitions and skating shows. In her senior year in high school, she auditioned for Ice Capades and Ice Follies, eventually choosing Ice Capades. Two weeks after high school graduation, she left home to begin training in Atlantic City. She remained with this traveling show for what would be a year-and-a-half stint. During her time with Ice Capades, they taped two television shows that aired over the holidays. After she left the life on the road, she attended Penn State and married a couple of years later. My dad, Mike, played for the Green Bay Packers in the 70s and Mom was able to do some coaching in the area while living there; however, having four children tabled most of her personal skating opportunities. For almost 40 years her skates were sidelined.

In 2010, Mom accompanied her sister, Monica, to the International Adult Figure Skating Championships in Oberstdorf, Germany, as her personal coach. My aunt, eight years her junior, was first taught how to skate by my mom on a homemade rink in their backyard in New York. Aunt Monica had continued to train through the years. Being

an observer at the event inspired my mom to contemplate returning to skating. Adult skaters from all over the world (ages 29–78)
come together each May and enjoy themselves by sharing their talents in singles, pairs, dance, and synchronized events. On September 16th, 2010, Mom stepped back on the ice with new skates and
began a most enjoyable and fulfilling season as an adult figure skater.
She relied on her memory to reeducate herself, keeping a journal
to chronicle her improvement and joy. Her goal was to compete in
the Oberstdorf competition in May 2011, so she needed to have
choreographed programs for both a freeskate and an artistic event.
She chose her music and began to choreograph her programs. Then
in January, her sister let her know she had a mere 30 days to prepare
for a competition taking place in Paris in March of 2011; my aunt felt
my mom needed a dress rehearsal before the big event in Germany.
Despite being small, the Paris competition was the perfect situation
for a 62-year-old embarking on her encore career! Mom did not
know how she would respond when her name was announced, but
she was pleasantly surprised by the lack of nerves and sense of complete joy she felt. The fact that her youngest child, the alien baby, was
in the audience was also a special treat. She won both of her events
and garnered the confidence to continue training for Oberstdorf.

When Mom returned home, she hired a coach to help her with the
technical aspects of her skating in order to better prepare her for
the International Championships in Oberstdorf. Her children and
grandchildren were all very excited about what she was doing. When
my aunt and mom left for Germany in May of 2011, they had three
daughters and two granddaughters join them. Her efforts awarded
her a second place in the artistic event and first place in the technical freeskate. She and my Aunt Monica became "Team Spalding"
in memory of their dad who died in 2001. He had been their driver
to early morning practices and their biggest cheerleader. He himself
had discovered a love of getting on the ice at a later age. When the

family moved to Erie, Pennsylvania, in the mid-60s, my grandfather started ice skating. Within a year, he had passed the initial level for dance from the United States Figure Skating Association. In order to pass, he needed to skate with a professional level figure skater, so my mom joyfully agreed to be his partner—all on his 50th birthday. He always told his daughters to "Live it up!" With their adult skating, they were beginning to do exactly that—living it up!

The goal to return annually to the International Championships motivated my mom to continue improving and begin working on more difficult elements for her programs, by adding more jumps and spins. With her coach's assistance, she slowly gained confidence with these new elements even though the muscle soreness and risk of falling increased. With two new programs in the works, my aunt and mom planned their 2012 competition schedule—adding an Easter weekend event in the Italian Alps followed by the next weekend in Paris to defend their titles. My mom chose the song "Amazing Grace" by Celtic Woman for her artistic program as a tribute to her dad. It was his favorite hymn. One month after these two events, they were in Germany for my mom's second and final appearance at the International Championships. This time she placed first in the artistic event and second in the technical freeskate. She had no idea that the soreness in her left quadriceps muscle would be diagnosed six weeks after returning home as a form of soft tissue sarcoma.

Sarcoma makes up about one percent of all cancer diagnoses in adults, with about 14,000 new cases each year. 23-percent of the time sarcomas are cured by surgery, 30-percent of the time by surgery with chemotherapy and/or radiation, and 50-percent of the time they are resistant to any form of treatment. My mom started feeling a soreness in her left thigh in March 2012. She thought she might have pulled something doing one of her sit spins, but the pain never went away—even with sport massage therapy. So after returning from Germany at the end of May 2012, she decided to have her leg examined by an orthopedic specialist. The doctor was convinced that it was a hematoma and scheduled an MRI for verification. On June 14th, 2012, the MRI was taken on what was now a lump in her thigh—something that started out as just a simple sore muscle. She was referred to an orthopedic oncologist, and he even thought it was a hematoma but decided to do a biopsy. On July 7th, 2012, Mom received the news that it was cancer.

This book is a compilation of my mom's journals—it starts with a brief section of journal entries where my mom tracks her return to skating. She called it her "Journal of a Comeback." But most specifically the book follows her entries from February 2012 to February 2013. These were the months leading up to and following her diagnosis. They focus primarily on her steadfast love for life, the insights, joy and wisdom she gained by spending time in the Word with her Father, and her enduring trust in God's sovereignty despite the news of her condition. I have given each month during that year its own chapter. Sprinkled in with these entries, I have also included some from Mom's earlier journals. Any journal dates that are bold and in block format were written outside the February 2012 to February 2013 time frame. I have chosen these earlier entries because they touch on notable themes that ran through Mom's journals—and her life. These themes include Mom's reflections on overcoming her first bout of cancer in 1997, her daddy, her grandmother and great-grandmother, her fascination with full moons, and her "happy room"—among others. Everything you will read is an entry from Mom's journals, with one exception—the "updates" I wrote to inform family and friends of my mom's progression during the cancer journey. These recount the information from the doctors and provide a little more depth from my perspective on caring for my mom. These entries do not begin until August 2012. They will be labeled as "Updates" and will, just as Mom's older journal entries, be bold and in block format.

I would also like to introduce you to our immediate family so that when you see a name, you will know to whom Mom is referring. In her journals, she writes excitedly about the faith heritage she received from her great-grandmother, Rose Secoy Moore, and she also highlights memories of her grandmother, Gladys Dowling. Both these women are linked to her through her mother's side of the family. Her parents, David and Rose Spalding, have four kids— Brian, Kiara (affectionately known as "Kia," my mom), Monica, and Kevin. My mom married Michael "Mike" McCoy. They too have four kids—Molly, Maggie, Katie, and Caleb (that's me, the alien baby). Molly and Jason Evans eloped, much to my mother's surprise, and they have been happily married for the past 18 years. They have four kids—Kylie, Kaitlyn, Karson, and Kasen, as well as a dog named Champ. Following the trend, Maggie and Jeff Henson eloped as well. They are both serving our country in the United States Army, have been happily married for two-and-a-half years and have a dog named Duke. Katie is Mom's only daughter to have had a proper wedding. She married Randy Barnett eight-and-a-half years ago, and they have three kids—Rody, Anna Kate, and David McCoy. They named David "Coy" for short, because Katie doesn't believe I will get married and have a son to pass along the family name. Of course, she is kidding. I think.

In August of 2012, I returned to the states from France, where I work at a Christian camp. It is a tradition for all of us to spend time together at the end of the summer at a family camp on Lake Erie. My parents could not make it that year, because my mom had just started radiation treatments. Things went downhill pretty quickly after that, and Dad asked me if I would stay home to be Mom's primary caregiver. My mom didn't want my dad to cancel his already booked schedule of speaking to students in Catholic Schools about the message of faith, hope and encouragement. I didn't hesitate to say yes. I cherish the time I spent with my mom—cooking for her, helping with physical therapy, and when she felt well enough, taking her for walks in her wheelchair during the last glimpses of daylight. The day she passed away my sister, Molly, speaking of me being the caregiver, told me, "It was supposed to be you." Up until that point, I had never really felt a purpose for my life. I never felt that I was doing something for which I was really passionate. My sister's statement hit me. *What if life didn't work out the way I thought because I was supposed to be there for my mom during that time?* All the times it hadn't worked out with a girl and then making the decision not to go to graduate school, perhaps happened for a reason. I wouldn't have been able to spend time with my mom if I had a family or if I had been in any other life situation. In the days following Mom's passing, as I began reading her journals and then decided to read selections during her celebration service, I knew I had to compile her writings into a book.

I know it was my mother's prayers that got me through many dark valleys and deep doubts. It is difficult not being able to talk to her every week when I would call her from France. The following is one of her prayers for me:

June 3ʳᵈ, 2003

As Caleb leaves today for Europe, I pray You open his eyes to the truth of who You've created him to be. Remember Lord, I did not ask You for this child—I did not even expect to have another—but You created him without any help from me. I know You have a unique plan for him as is evident in the way You have made him. I pray You give him new eyes as he sees new sights in Your creation. I pray You grow his roots deeper into the understanding of Your love and the amazing power You have gifted him with. Meet the

*longings of his heart as he trusts in You. May he see
signs of Your goodness everywhere he goes and when
he returns to us in six weeks, he'll have renewed hope
and sense of purpose!*

As you read this book, my mom's journals, my prayer for you is that your roots would grow deeper in the understanding of God's love for you. Regardless of your background and the battles you are facing right now, may you fully trust in God's sovereignty for your life.

journal of a comeback— skating reflections

July 2010

After "coaching" Monica at the World Championships in Oberstdorf in May, I was encouraged to get back on the ice myself. Why? These "adult" skaters have so much fun doing something they thoroughly enjoy. I might enjoy it too. It's great exercise in a cool location, good for balance, and I'd be using a skill I already have, though a bit rusty—actually 35 years rusty! Step one, skates needed. I do own skates but my feet have changed sizes. It will be a significant investment. Skates first became part of my life when I was five or six as I skated on Cooper's Pond in the winter. Thinking of all these hours on the ice with lessons, practice, tests, and competitions. Ice Capades. So here I am at 61.5 years old getting back on the ice after at least 30 years—more like 35 years. Surely this will be a good workout and good for balance, right? I have no idea what to expect, but I suspect my daddy is smiling at the attempt! With the financial investment made, step one of the process is done. I have no idea where to go from here, but it will be one step at a time. To God be the Glory!

November 3rd, 2010

Caleb brought my camera—good grief—and shot some video that should help. And he sat on the spot where he broke his leg, 7-13-96, over 14 years ago. It changed the path of his life in many ways.

November 18th, 2010

It's been two months since I first got back on the ice. I do feel stronger and more secure and less like I have to micro manage every move, but I still have a long way to go. There is an inner joy and enjoyment as I move across the ice from fond memories, years of hard work, and a sense that my daddy would be delighting in what I am doing. He did enjoy his skating and I'm so grateful for the lessons learned from him in that department as well.

Live it up!! While you can.

January 7th, 2011

The public session at 10 a.m. was a bit more crowded than I would like, but a good workout. I'm trying to do more reps of my jumps, building up strength and confidence. Sharon the Vet was there and she said she thinks I can do the competition. Then Cathy came in with her kids—what a sweet treat to see her and them. Sweet Joe the zamboni man celebrating five years of colon-cancer-free living. Monica wrote about a competition in Paris in March. It would be fun to do since it would be on our Dad's 90th birthday—ten years after he died. I read over the requirements for Oberstdorf and it was encouraging as it wasn't as tough as I thought.

Onward!

January 9th, 2011

I'm wearing this cozy chenille jacket I got for my birthday in 2001, ten years ago, just before my dad died. Oh the memory, how he opened his eyes when I walked in and showed it to him—kiss on the cheek. How I treasure that memory.

Now ten years later and I'm skating and enjoying it because I know he would, and grateful You gave me the talent and the opportunity as a child to learn such a graceful sport. I really do ask that as I go forward with my plans that You would direct my steps. That what I do honors You and honors his memory and advice. Live it up! Ten years ago I never would have imagined I'd be where I am in this, having fun and back on the ice.

January 18th, 2011

I am downloading music and praying for inspiration. I want to honor God and my dad's memory in everything I do with this.

February 4ᵗʰ, 2011

Haven't felt well all week but decided to skate anyway. It was a good 50 minutes of just skating with jumps, spins, and footwork. Everything felt good. Tried some inside brackets and will incorporate that in footwork. It was a good session and I thought about how 14 years ago it was the day before my cancer surgery and how the future looked unclear. Now here I am at 61 doing this and having fun.

March 8ᵗʰ, 2011

My last birthday I could never have imagined where I would be on my 62ⁿᵈ birthday. Now I'm off to foreign lands with my skates, music, costumes, and everything else needed for competition. Crazy!

March 11ᵗʰ, 2011

So much has happened since our last travel in May 2010. I started back on the ice after ordering skates and blades on September 16ᵗʰ. Here I am for our Tenth Anniversary David Spalding Memorial Trip and would he ever love this one!

Both of Dave's girls are competing in the Coupe de France in Paris March 19ᵗʰ and 20ᵗʰ on what would have been his 90ᵗʰ birthday.

March 16th, 2011

Six months ago today I stepped on the ice for the first time in 34 years with new skates. Now here I am on my way to Paris to compete. What in the world!

March 19th, 2011

I skated second after Christine. I loved it. No nerves, just fun. I couldn't understand a word because it was all in French.

I received many compliments afterward, many of which I couldn't understand. Caleb was so nervous and he got teary seeing me out there.

What's up with that?

April 12th, 2011

Here we go! My first official lesson in probably 46 years. 36 dollars for 30 minutes. I didn't do much skating, just talked through stuff and strategized. He watched my jumps. I tried a loop and got a physics lesson on jumps and spins. I can see he's very serious about skating and I do appreciate that. I'm sure he's trying to figure me out.

"What is she doing and why?" he's probably wondering. It'll be interesting . . .

May 18th, 2011

Thank You for this day, Lord, for all Your blessings. I am loved! I've been thinking about the past eight months since I've been back on the ice . . . how it wasn't a goal or even a desire of mine yet it has taken on an interesting life, how revisiting skills learned a long time ago has given me joy, but not just to me, my husband, my mother, my sister, my children and grandchildren, my friends, my skating cohorts, my coach, my surgeon.

All these years of raising kids, working at the bank, caring for my dying daddy, and here I am 14 years after a cancer diagnosis and surgery, preparing to go on an international competition in Germany! And having one of my daughters and my oldest grandchild, my sister, two nieces and a great niece all being there!

Sharon the Vet saying, "You're living the life I want." Help me to do my best and enjoy all the steps along the way. I think my desire in all of this is to enjoy this gift You've given me. To honor my daddy's memory by doing something he would love and to bring You glory through the interactions with family and friends. It's really not about me; it's what You are doing through this opportunity to enrich my life and the lives of those dear to me.

Reflecting on Isaiah 55—how I prayed for a hunger and thirst for Your Word years ago, and how now I crave this time with You, just letting Your Word have its profound effect in my heart, soul, and mind. Over time, how You continue to teach me, just as I sit here with my coffee in this little corner of Your amazing creation. And along the way You continue to delightfully surprise me with treasures.

May 20th, 2011

Two weeks until we leave for Germany. I was just sitting here again thinking how one year ago today Monica and I were finishing our time in Oberstdorf and I was beginning to think about getting back on the ice. Now here I am, beyond what I could have asked or imagined, feeling ready to go, confidently performing two programs, and bringing my daughter and granddaughter with me. I just never would have thought, but thank You for allowing me to have this fun. And I continue to ask that I honor You in all I do.

June 9th, 2011

Competition Skate! I skated second of the first group with 13 skaters in all. Our group had a little cheer before we took the ice for warm up. "Have fun!" The crowd was great, very enthusiastic and encouraging. Everything went well except at the end when I got a little turned around but I was happy. I placed second behind Barbara from Canada by less than a point. It was so much fun. Rhea came up to me before the award to shake my hand and compliment my skate. And Marina gave me my award and she too complimented my program. And the photographer said he got some great shots that I need to see.

September 6th, 2011

What a weekend! Filled with activity with family and the Peach Classic. I find myself asking, "Did this really happen?"

Some sweet memories:
- Skating with my sister
- Seeing Sharon skate her first competition event and seeing her men there to support her!
- Mike being there and his great photography
- Having four generations of family in the crowd
- Yes, Rose D. Spalding was in the house 9-4-11, 89 years old.
- Bowing to her before we skated
- Anna Kate and Rody's wide-eyed wonder
- Hearing AK yell, "Grandma!"
- "Grandma you have nice legs." (Rody) Actually, it was the tights.
- Coming in 2nd to a monkey!
- Kevin, Monica, and I all together
- Karin and Gary watching and bringing flowers—so sweet.

The amazement that a year ago I wasn't even on the ice, and now my world is full of skating experiences, three competitions, new friends, and enjoyment.

It's given me and Monica something to do together in addition to our memorial trips where we can honor our daddy's memory with an activity he so enjoyed.

Thank You, Father, for this gift!

December 1st, 2011

I was on the ice at 8:20 and started the lesson at 8:40. We talked about music and program content. I worked on sit spin and took away the crutch of left hand on knee. Triggers are to apex both arms and free leg, scoop upward to finish. Flip-pull arms in, leaving space. Take time to let free leg reach into ice. We'll plan to meet again next Thursday and maybe have music. Monica and I talked about a competition in Italy in April.

Let's go!

January 6th, 2012

It was so fun working with Davin on my program yesterday. It was a new experience for me. The strategy and planning was all very interesting. I do love the "Amazing Grace" music and I pray for Your guidance there as I prepare to skate to it in honor of my daddy. I want it to honor his memory as the message of John Newton's hymn was so dear to him. I pray that the true message comes through and that somehow I will have the opportunity to speak the truth about its message in my skating and to those I'm with as to why I chose it and exactly what it means and the grace offered to every sinner even to those at the Ice Forum as I prepare.

January 9th, 2012

I had the ice all to myself because Georgia got new skates and was taking a break. I feel so blessed. Worked on footwork ideas, loop entrance, and camel-sit combo. Not only am I almost 63, but I have my own ice surface! I am getting spoiled. I need to remember to bring my music into the rink. I skated in silence but it was still very good.

January 30th, 2012

Played my music and it was awesome. I'm still waiting for inspiration with "Amazing Grace." It is such wonderful music and words. Brings tears to my eyes.

february 2012

February 5th, 2012

Celebrating the 15th anniversary of being cancer-free, and full of praise and thanksgiving and amazement that You spared my life when I was in the trenches and have allowed me these years of life and journey with You to know the love that surpasses knowledge. To enjoy six grandchildren's lives, to travel with Monica to places our dad would have loved, to return to skating and enjoy its benefits. This is a day to be celebrated as I reflect on Your goodness to me!

Thank You for every day, every step, and every memory. You are my awesome God and I have seen Your goodness in the land of the living.

February 6th, 2012

The start of another week at home—I am so grateful!

Fifteen years ago I was told, "I was so lucky" that the cancer was found because my symptoms didn't warrant the biopsy that the doctor performed. You, Lord, were giving wisdom. I was so preoccupied with my dad in a nursing home, Molly trying to get into physician's assistant school, Katie a high school senior trying to decide on a college, Caleb just a sophomore, Mike on the road, and my leave of absence from First Union—my goodness! You will keep him in perfect peace whose mind is stayed on You. And You did and continue to do so.

I was thinking today about Caleb's question asked by his coach, "What is your biggest fear?" As I've been meditating on that I realize with You I have nothing to fear. Honestly, anything that comes to mind quickly fades in the light of Your presence. You have overcome the world and I can be of good cheer. It's my choice. I can always choose to worry, but delighting myself in You has proven to be my safe place, knowing Your life that surpasses knowledge.

Bless my family today, and open their eyes to see it is from You!

February 5th, 2001

Praise to You alone as I celebrate four years of cancer-free living! I know it was You who led the doctor to do the biopsy and I thank You for Your guiding hand through the subsequent events. Indeed Your hand has been on me, and I give You the glory. Great things You have done.

Dad looks so pitiful and so near the end of his earthly life. Oh, that You would take him soon. Jesus, You hold the key to death and I trust You to deliver him to Your kingdom of light and life safely!

February 6th, 2005

February 6th, 2005

Yesterday, I sensed that there was something special about the day, but didn't realize until late that it was the eighth anniversary of my cancer surgery.

Just as You instructed the Israelites in Exodus 23:14 to celebrate three times each year in Your honor, because of Your faithfulness to them, I celebrate Your faithfulness to me and remember Your goodness. In these eight years, You have given me a hunger and thirst for Your Word, shown me the treasures of darkness as I ministered to my dying earthly father, celebrated his life through my trips with Monica, three grandchildren, 2,922 mornings of new mercies, and many rich memories and friendships because of Your faithfulness.

That event eight years ago helped get me off the treadmill of the world's success path and into deep study of Your Word. During that time I was disappointed about not being blessed to minister to Marlene, but doubly blessed to minister to Susan and my daddy as they left the earth.

Looking back, I thought I had a clue, but what I've learned in these years has given me reason to boast! I do know and understand You so much better, and I know that, like 2 Corinthians 2:14 says, You always lead in triumphal procession in Christ and spread everywhere the fragrance of the knowledge of You!

February 5ᵗʰ, 2007

Glory to You, LORD! All day I've been celebrating Your goodness to me as ten years ago was my cancer surgery, remembering the bafflement of the doctors and the blessing to know You worked through them to protect me.

And I was just thinking of some of the blessings I've experienced over these ten years and how You have taught me of Yourself.

- Katie and Caleb graduate from high school.
- Molly, PA school; Katie, Maggie, and Caleb all college graduates; Katie master's degree
- First grandchild and being able to develop a relationship with her from the very beginning!
- Another granddaughter in 2000
- Grandson in 2002
- Ministering to Susan as she entered Your rest 10-10-2000. That was preparation for the experience with Dad! And being with him as he entered Your rest—3-22-01.
- Working with Mike in ministry
- Bible studies personally with Braves' wives, GCC (Gwinnett Community Church) Women, and Falcons' wives

- Trips with Monica in Dad's memory to Ireland, Czech, Italy, France, Nationals, and Olympics
- Family reunions in Wisconsin and Poland
- Grandma Moore's Bible!
- Katie's wedding, Romans 8:38-39
- NCAA Championships at Stanford
- Olympic Trials in Sacramento
- Camp Fitch, watching all three grandchildren ride bikes
- Help me to proclaim Your faithfulness, that my heart, O Lord my God, will give You thanks forever!

February 4th, 2009

Twelve years ago today I was facing cancer surgery not knowing what would be found nor what the prognosis would be. I remember saying, *You will keep [me] in perfect peace [if my mind] is steadfast, because [I] trust in You (Isaiah 26:3).*

You are a faithful God! All that I have experienced in these twelve years is a gift from You.

February 5th, 2011

A Day of Remembrance! It was 14 years ago today that I had surgery for uterine cancer and the doctor told me I was "lucky" because it was discovered when it was. I remember saying Isaiah 26:3 over and over as I went into surgery, not knowing what they would find.

I praise You, Lord, for Your goodness to me. It was in the middle of one of the most difficult times of my life, as I was on a leave of absence from my bank job due to the issues with my dad's health. Two kids still at home, Mike with Bill Glass, and daily phone calls with mother. So much of life I've lived and enjoyed in these 14 years, and I'm grateful for every day of it. You didn't have to give me one day, but you've given me over 5,100 of them since that day. And now I'm back skating, crazy as that sounds. I have six grandchildren, all of my four kids have graduated from college, I've been so many places around the world and seen so many things. Dad has been in Your presence about ten years now, and I got to be with him as he left this earth. I've served at Missionary Refresh three times and I am so blessed; Lee Ling's story still amazes me. Celebrated 40 years of marriage, Mike's now in the Philippines—amazing stuff!!

I do want to spend this day deliberately and constantly thanking You for all You've given me—not just in the last 14 years, although that is my focus. It's a good day!

February 9th, 2012

Earlier on the ice today I overheard a discussion between Julie and Sarah. Julie's church had a twenty-minute service last night and there was some puzzle about what the celebration was. Julie goes to a Universalist Church. Sarah asked if that is "Christian" and her answer was: "Not per se, but most of the members have come from bad experiences in Christian denominations."

I am so sorry. Forgive us, Lord, for making "religion" such a bad experience in our efforts to follow Jesus.

May You continue to guide those whose hearts are bent on following and loving You to find truth apart from what their churches are teaching.

Help us, Lord, to see through the distractions and come to the place of truly knowing You and enjoying Your presence.

Lisa told me how much she enjoyed working with me. Last week her mother commented on her disposition when she came home and she told her she just had the best lesson with a new student. I thought she was going to cry! The message of Dad's favorite "Amazing Grace" continues to bless others. Thank You, Lord.

Psalm 32:7-8
You are my hiding place; you will protect me from trouble and surround me with songs of deliverance. I will instruct you and teach you in the way you should go; I will counsel you and watch over you.

February 11th, 2012

I have been praying for Laura. You know her needs and her deepest need. Continue to meet her where she is and restore her faith and fill her with all spiritual wisdom and understanding that only Your power can provide.

Exodus 33:14
You said to Moses, *"My Presence will go with you, and I will give you rest."*

Exodus 33:15-16

Moses' reply: *"If your Presence does not go with us, do not send us up from here. . . . What else will distinguish me and your people from all the other people on the face of the earth?"*

Your presence in me distinguishes me from "the world," and Your presence gives me rest in the midst of all that is going on around me.

Psalm 33:10-11

The LORD foils the plans of the nations; he thwarts the purposes of the peoples. But the plans of the LORD stand firm forever, the purposes of his heart through all generations.

This is such a good and timely reminder as I look at this world—turmoil in the Middle East, concern for America, You are in control.

Always have been.

Always will be.

Thank You, Father that I can know this—know *You*—and trust You to be faithful to Your Word.

February 14th, 2012

Thank You for that special encounter with Natalie yesterday in Sam's. Continue to strengthen and encourage her as she raises those kids in Mark's absence. She is such a dear!

February 15th, 2012

Thank You for the gift of today—a day at home, alone with You, just time to catch up on things on my list and to enjoy the quiet peace. Mike is in California. Thank You for surrounding him with Your favor yesterday—a $400 Delta credit plus a first-class seat on the next flight which worked better for the guy picking him up. Oh, the amazing ways You bless us!

February 16th, 2012

Mark 1:40
The leper said to Jesus, *"If you are willing, you can make me clean."*

If You are willing, if it is for Your good, You can. You are able to do anything. Direct my steps today. May the words of my mouth and the meditations of my heart be pleasing to You. Give me strength for the tasks ahead. Let me be a blessing at the rink and with Sindhu and Valen.

Thank You for the good news for Sindhu that she doesn't have to be on complete bed rest, no premature labor signs, that baby A and baby B are doing well and developing normally.

Continue to bless that sweet family, and remind her of Your faithfulness any time she's prone to worry.

February 18th, 2012

So nice to just lay in bed this morning, and I realize it's been four days since I've had the TV on, enjoying getting back to reading

The Story of Civilization by Durrant—covered Augustine and Saint Patrick this week. They lived such a long time ago but someday I will meet them, and so many more heroes of the faith.

Meditating on Psalm 33.

Psalm 33:18
The eyes of the LORD are on those who fear him, on those whose hope is in his unfailing love, to deliver them from death and keep them alive in famine.

February 24th, 2012

Today I leave for South Carolina and North Carolina for five days of grandkid time. I do thank You for each of these six precious ones, and their parents. As Mike goes to Chicago for the "Faith" Hall of Fame, give him opportunities to share about Your amazing grace and unfailing love that will connect with the hearts of the hearers. Thank You for the opportunities You provide, the doors You open, and the ability to see Your hand and heart at work.

I enjoyed my talk with Lisa yesterday as she helped me put the finishing touches on "Amazing Grace." Bless her with some rest.

February 26th, 2012

At the Barnetts', leaving for the Evans' today. What a treat yesterday was, having time with Katie to shop a bit, and a couple of fun hours with the kids while Katie and Randy got out. We rode the horsey, played in the tree, had pizza and oranges, danced and spun. I will treasure the memory of the looks of delight on their faces. And Anna Kate as we rocked before bed, she sang the words to "Jesus loves me" with me. Lord, bless her with the understanding of Your love for her throughout her life.

march 2012

March 1st, 2012

Thank You again, Lord, for a safe journey, time with the grandkids—
memories! Back home for a few days with plenty to do. Enjoying the
blessing of memorizing Psalm 33, and the wonderful reminders of
Your faithfulness, justice, righteousness, and power. You are worthy
to be praised.

March 4th, 2012

Celebrated Mary Smith's life yesterday with the Crossans, Dave
Ferrante's 50th with family and friends, and hosted Kevin and
Martin overnight. Now Mike is off to D. C. and I get to wrap up things
before heading to North Carolina for some one-on-one time with Kasen.

It's all good and I'm so grateful for life and time with others that You allow me to enjoy!

March 6th, 2012

Off to North Carolina today to spend some time with Kasen while the rest of his family goes to D. C. Thankful You have provided this opportunity for all of us.

And thanks for the reminder from Romans 8 on Sunday.

Romans 8:5
Those who live according to the sinful nature have their minds set on what that nature desires; but those who live in accordance with the Spirit have their minds set on what the Spirit desires.

Setting the mind is intentional. I can't expect an unredeemed person to be thinking the way I do when my mind is set on You.

"I am ruled and determined by His awakening, regenerating, illuminating presence characterized by the fact that He *indwells* me."
—H.C.G Moule (source unknown)

Give Randy and Esther good times of refreshment as they travel and spend time in Florida. Keep their focus on You and Your assurance of continued faithfulness.

March 7th, 2012

10:30—Kasen napping. It's a little bit off-schedule but a good morning nonetheless.

Thanks for the shield of protection as I traveled yesterday—flight delay, plane and gate change, after-dark arrival, and trip to Roxboro in my fancy black rental.

And thanks for this time of quiet to spend in Your Word. Keep me strong and alert as I care for this precious child. Thank You for this time. And help those in D. C. to have a good and educational time.

March 8ᵗʰ, 2012

My 63ʳᵈ birthday and spending it with sweet Kasen, a good night's sleep. He's watching "Madagascar." We are becoming such good friends. Thank You for this treasure, a delightful birthday gift from You.

The rest of the family had a good time in D. C. yesterday. What a treat for them to have this experience up close.

I do pray for all those battling illnesses and their families, and for Donna Greason and the others from GCC saying farewell to loved ones. You are faithful to comfort if we just let You.

March 9ᵗʰ, 2001

Yesterday, was very special—a beautiful day, clear and warm, trees still flowering. And I was able to take a long afternoon walk and enjoy the beauty of creation. I felt like it was God's gift to me! My early morning with my dad—how tender as I told him it was March 8ᵗʰ. He knew it was my day, and he gave me a strong kiss on my right cheek. *Wow*!

March 8th, 2004

Today I celebrate 55 years of physical life and I awake today from a beautiful mountain cabin in Cleveland, Georgia, praising You for Your faithfulness to me! One of the best two of my birthdays was spent in England with Monica—last year running out of gas driving Dan's car! And the other was three years ago. I remember visiting my near-death daddy at the nursing home and telling him it was a beautiful day in Georgia—a ten on the Mellish meter! Those words caused him to force open his eyes and acknowledge that March 8th was a special day to him. He planted a firm kiss on my right cheek. It brought me to tears then, and now as I remember the event, I realize that was the last kiss he ever was able to give me. Fourteen days later he slipped peacefully into Your presence forever.

As we arrived here last night to discover our accommodations by the river wouldn't be available, our host gave us the keys to the newly-completed "Top of the Morn" cabin which faces east over the mountains. John Lance's prayer was that You would give me a birthday to remember. And as we returned to the cabin after dinner in Helen, the full moon was rising between the clouds. For almost an hour, in silence, we watched it rise as I kept Psalm 19 in my mind. This was a gift from You—priceless! Thank You. "What did you get for your birthday, Kia?" How could I put into words Your goodness to me?

The Scripture today is Numbers 10 and 11—Moses' prayer: *"Rise up, O LORD! May your enemies be scattered; may your foes flee before you"* (Numbers 10:35).

Wherever You lead, let me not forget it is You who goes before me clearing the way that I may see You!

March 8th, 2008

Today I celebrate the completion of 59 years on this earth. As I consider my journey, I am so grateful for Your goodness. And I chuckle as I read Numbers 11 again on the schedule for today and thank You for how it makes me laugh. I can't wait to thank Moses for including this part of his story in writing if only for my benefit. How often I say "enough" before the job is finished. Moses hit You with question after question and after You told him what You would do, he gives his analysis of the situation. How many times have I grumbled about a situation and given You my analysis? Please don't answer that. You are who You say You are and I desire to exercise that present active-participle faith.

March 9th, 2012

Another good night of sleep. This has been such a blessing. Kasen is really doing well—amazing. We went to Golden Corral yesterday for lunch with the church ladies. It was fun to see them and get out for a bit.

Day three begins with the return of the family expected tonight. Thanks for protecting us as You so faithfully do, and giving me such sweet memories with my youngest grandbaby.

Hopefully he'll remember me fondly. Even if not, I have treasured memories of a special child at my "favorite" age—16 months.

As the group goes to the White House today, open their eyes to absorb the richness of the history they are in the presence of.

March 10ᵗʰ, 2003

The highlight of the trip to Prague was meeting Vesna after she discovered Leonard Rotter's paintings in her shop. What an amazing story. Her friend Romana (age 72)—the daughter of Leonard—was cleaning out her house and discovered a suitcase with 31 watercolor paintings left by her father which he painted between 1948-1963. Vesna is going to do a gallery exhibit of this famous sculptor's paintings that he did in his final years around Prague. Now Monica and I each have two paintings and a connection with another daughter who desires to honor her departed father.

What a treasure to have a piece of history that had been hidden for forty years in a suitcase! It makes me wonder if all these years it was saved there just for us— oh, I know it was. A Jewish artist born in 1895, a history of creative pursuits and accomplishments now finds a home in Georgia. And how significant this makes me feel that God would bless us in this special way in His timing.

March 12th, 2012

Reminder of Romans 2:4
Do you show contempt for the riches of his kindness, tolerance and patience, not realizing that God's kindness leads you toward repentance?

As I am reading Numbers 14:11:
When you asked Moses, *"How long will these people treat me with contempt? How long will they refuse to believe in me, in spite of the miraculous signs I have performed among them?"*

This is after Joshua and Caleb gave the good report about the land and the other spies grumbled. The minority opinion. Then Moses gives his plea before You, which reveals his understanding of You.

Numbers 14:19
"In accordance with your great love, forgive the sin of these people, just as you have pardoned them from the time they left Egypt until now."

Numbers 14:23
You forgive but, *"Not one of them will ever see the land I promised on oath to their forefathers. No one who has treated me with contempt will ever see it."*

Showing contempt by unbelief has consequences. Perhaps to avoid this You instructed us to "remember Your faithfulness" by intentionally celebrating times of remembrance.

And this coupled with Paul's words in Romans about judgment of others shows contempt for the riches of Your kindness. Tolerance and patience that I have received from You. The plank in my own eye.

But for Your amazing grace, and mercy, kindness, tolerance and patience with me, there is no imagining where I'd be today.

March 17th, 2012

A busy week, and now a couple days to rest. Thank You for yesterday morning's extended time with You, giving me the freedom to choose my practice time so I could just take my time with You to start my day. It was such a gift.

As I continue to learn and meditate on Psalm 33, I am so blessed by Your Word through the pen of David. Those twenty-two verses are so rich, expressing so much of what is on my heart these days. It is such a comfort as I think about all that is going on in the world— Jeff in Afghanistan where things are so unstable. I do trust Your protection of him and all our military.

And as I continue to read *The Story of Civilization*, I am reminded that there is indeed nothing new under the sun. Nations and leaders rise and fall, people do noble things and atrocious things.

You alone are the only constant. You speak and it comes to be. You command and it stands firm.

Psalm 33:11
The plans of the LORD stand firm forever, the purposes of his heart through all generations.

You are patient and tolerant beyond comprehension and I can't fathom how You delay Your return. Whenever it will be, what a glorious day!

March 19th, 2012

So grateful for my daddy today on the 91st anniversary of his birth. I felt his presence as I practiced today. It was all good.

March 20th, 2012

I was mindful throughout yesterday that it was the 91st anniversary of my daddy's birth, and how thankful I was for him. It was a good day. I got a lot done, had a good skate.

I do pray for calmness for my mother who has worked herself up over this extraction tomorrow. Maybe she's just gun shy, but she's very "worried." Maybe I could offer to pray with her.

March 21st, 2012

Today Rose has her dental procedures. You know the details of the day ahead. And Your grace is sufficient. I'm thankful for the reminder on Sunday as Steve Watts taught from Micah.

Micah 6:3
You asked: *"My people, what have I done to you? How have I burdened you?"*

You have showed me what is good and what You require. So act justly love mercy and walk humbly with your God.

You delight to show mercy! And so often we show contempt for that mercy by demanding something else—our comfort, happiness, desires. Forgive us, Lord. Forgive me, Lord.

Thank You for satisfying my desires with good things so my youth is renewed. You are amazing, God, and I stand in awe of You.

March 22ⁿᵈ, 2012

The 11ᵗʰ Anniversary of Dad's home going. Reflecting on the special memories surrounding that special time, grateful for yesterday's success with mother. What would she do without me? Obviously You orchestrated this plan and have been faithful each step of the way. Talk about never imagining? Her gratitude and the impact of the prayer yesterday by Dr. Satterfield!

January 24ᵗʰ, 2001

11:20 p.m.
As I sit and rehearse Your faithfulness, O God, I am so completely confident in Your sovereignty. I contemplate it now as I consider the possibility of my daddy's life coming to an end on this earth. I praise You who is the Author and Finisher of life. Nothing happens apart from Your plan and I am so grateful that You have made Yourself known to me—that brings me comfort. Let me rest in the shadow of Your almighty Presence and be real to my dad as he sleeps and remove any fear or anxiety he may have tonight.

May my words and the meditations of my heart be pleasing to You my God, my rock, and my redeemer.

March 10th, 2001

I have such a clear memory of some 17-18 years ago at Presque Isle when Dad and I ran a 10k race. He was about the last to finish, for heaven's sake. He was over 60 and I cheered as he neared the finish line. Here I am again as Dad is finishing his earthly race and I'm on the finish line encouraging him, and as he did in that 10K race. I want to see his victor's smile and when I finish my race I'll rejoice to see his face as one of a great cloud of witnesses!

March 23rd, 2001

I see Your character consistent in the life of my dad. How he rejoiced to see me every time I visited and hated to see me leave and always expressed his appreciation! How he said he didn't want strangers orchestrating his final symphony. What You have prepared for those who love You, Lord, was evident last night.

Numbers 6:24-26
"The LORD bless you and keep you; the LORD make his face shine upon you and be gracious unto you; the LORD turn his face toward you and give you peace."

I kiss him. Bye-bye, Daddy. Softly, quietly he leaves.

June 20th, 2004

It's Father's Day and I'm so blessed as I came across some of my dad's words from March 1997. In response to, "I love you, Dad," he would say:

"I love you too, I am so lucky."
"And me thee."
"You can't come close to my love for you."
And as I say "I love You, Lord," I know I can't come close to Your love for me. Thank You for Jesus and the cross that demonstrates Your love!

March 14th, 2008

Seven years ago I was earnestly praying, as my earthly father lay dying, that You would orchestrate his passing into glory in a way that would be special, as only You can do.

What You did was marvelous!

March 19th, 2008

I'll make a cake today, my dad's favorite—white with chocolate frosting. He would have been 87, You gave him 80 years and three days to "live it up" and as I reflect on Your working in his final days, I think how now seven years later, we are again waiting but now for a life to begin.

January 4ᵗʰ, 2010

Thankful for the tender reminder yesterday at GCC as we sang "Amazing Grace." The memories of my daddy who is now in Your presence having been brought there by Your grace. His stains are gone; he has been set free! May Your precious Word dwell in me so I will be equipped for every situation by Your grace, I pray.

March 19ᵗʰ, 2010

89 years ago today my earthly daddy was born and nine years ago today we made his final birthday cake—his favorite white cake with chocolate frosting. He didn't eat it, but we celebrated anyway. Three days later he entered Your presence. Lots of memories—sweet memories of that time. I thank You for that!

It's good to remember and reflect but the only thing that matters is what I do with my *now*.

March 23ʳᵈ, 2012

Yesterday, was such a sweet day. No sense of urgency with time to reflect periodically on that date eleven years ago as I spent time with Dad until he entered eternity with You! Thank You.

Such a sweet time talking with Katie last night and hearing the improvement in her outlook . . . with her weight, the kids, the house, and the land. It's all good. Can Rody really be turning four? How he has filled my life with joy!

And tonight I fly to Colorado to spend the weekend with Maggie—how fun! Thank You for this special blessing.

March 24th, 2012

In Colorado, 6,000 feet, a beautiful morning! All went well in my trip.

Again I remember Amos 4:13.
He who forms the mountains, creates the wind, and reveals his thoughts to man, he who . . . treads the high places of the earth—the LORD God almighty is his name.

These mountains are beautiful, and those who live here, though they see them every day, do they think of who formed them?

March 25th, 2012

A delightful day yesterday, just being with Maggie, shopping and talking, dinner and the Irish dancers. Thank You for the gift!

Thoughts from today's reading:
By the way, I do love Deuteronomy!

Deuteronomy 4:27, 29-31
You made clear what would happen if Israel became corrupt.

Only a few of you will survive among the nations to which the Lord will drive you. . . . But if from there you seek the LORD your God, you will find him if you look for him with all your heart and with all your soul. When you are in distress and all these things have happened to you, then in later days you will return to the LORD *you God and obey him. For the* LORD *your God is a merciful God; he will not abandon or destroy you.*

Oh, the reminders of Your mercy. As an example to me and the countless times You have been faithful not to abandon me and to continue to display Your patient mercy! I am so grateful.

When a man hears Your words and puts them into practice, he is like a man who builds a house on a solid foundation. When the torrent struck, it could not be shaken. But the one who hears and doesn't put into practice is like a man who doesn't even build on a foundation. The moment the torrent strikes, it collapsed and destruction was complete.

Every thought captive to Christ.

Psalm 68:3-4
May the righteous be glad and rejoice before God; may they be happy and joyful. Sing to God, sing praise to his name . . . his name is the LORD—*and rejoice before him.*

March 27th, 2012

Back home safely. Grateful for the gift of the time with Maggie. Thank You for her, for providing for her, protecting her and faithfully making her into a special thirty-six year old who has overcome so much and has so much to give. Continue to bless her and remind her of Your love for her.

Deuteronomy 5:29

You told Moses: *"Oh, that their hearts would be inclined to fear me and keep my commandments always, so that it might go well with them and their children forever."*

Keep my heart inclined in the special ways that You do!

March 28ᵗʰ, 2012

Grateful Mike is home safely after nine days on the road.

Sweet time encouraging Peggy yesterday—oh, the emotions of mothers and grandmothers. You know. Continue to comfort her in her disappointment and remind her that You indeed are sovereign in everything. Her desire to build into her granddaughter's life will look a little different then she first expected, but it can be done.

Thank You for the reminder of the ways You have provided for me to be a grandmother to my geographically-distant grandchildren.

March 30ᵗʰ, 1983

I want to be more consistent in recording my prayers and thoughts, Lord, because it helps me remember the feeling and the answers I experience. You know how tedious these days are with hardly time for myself. So help me to record these things for my own benefit. It was so good to review my prayers of the summer of 1978. Lord, You are consistently faithful. And how I recorded my enjoyment of the chosen people's journey from the Old Testament back in December 1980. Lord, You were preparing us for our Caleb. How really special this is—thank You!

March 31ˢᵗ, 2012

Last day of the month, 31 years ago, the last day of my final pregnancy and my unexpected boy turns 31 tomorrow. As he's like Caleb, following You wholeheartedly in his own way. Running his race, and I'm delighted with him knowing his heart is longing after You.

Just reflecting this morning as I prepare to leave tomorrow for England to skate in two competitions, Italy and France. To be with Monica, my dear, crazy sister. To have time with my oldest grandchild Kylie in Paris, with Caleb, my youngest child, as well as Laura, Crista, and Zoe.

Thinking of my earthly daddy and how when I asked him as I was pushing his wheelchair if he was afraid to die and he responded, "No, it's just that this is not what I expected to be doing at this point in my life." Age 75.

And here I am, feeling like he's asking me the same questions, and no, Dad, this is not what I expected to be doing at 63, not that I really had expectations like you did. But here I am, competing internationally with Monica, accompanied by children and grandchildren, driving to the rink in your 1990 Camry, reading *The Story of Civilization* by Durrant. Skating to "Could Have Danced All Night" and "Amazing Grace"—both in honor of you.

Rolling out the new "Team Spalding" shirts. Dave's girls. Honoring his memory. "Living it up."

I'm about bursting with amazement and joy!

Maybe part of it is God's abundance for giving my time to you as you spent the final years of your life in a nursing home. How He's opened the windows of heaven where He has you safely resting and poured abundant blessings on me, even now underwriting much of the financial piece.

I stand amazed and awed at God's goodness, for every good and perfect gift is from Him.

Kind of busy day ahead. Savoring the time in Your Word, enjoying Your presence and reminders of Your unfailing love.

april 2012

April 3rd, 2012

From High Wycombe, grateful for safe passage. It's a beautiful morning after a good night's sleep. Ready to hit the ice today on this side of the pond.

My soul has been consciously savoring Your mercy and grace in the recent days as I am humbly aware of Your amazing goodness to me—all I have, all that I am, all that You're doing. All that I can say is *wow* and thank You! Not just for being God in my life and doing what You alone do, but opening my eyes to see and appreciate, for giving me an awareness of Your presence. Your Word is not without effect! The blessings as I continue to memorize and meditate on Psalm 33, the impact it's having now, when I remember the impact verse 11 had so many years ago. But in context, it has so much more.

Luke 10:18-19
Jesus replied, *"I have given you authority . . . Do not rejoice that the spirits submit to you, but rejoice that your names are written in heaven."*

This says to me: Don't put your confidence or sense of worth in your "ministry" or calling, but in that my name is written in heaven. When I do what You have created me to do, I feel Your pleasure. And from the words of Jesus I know that it was for Your good pleasure that You reveal Yourself to those who come to You in childlike faith and teachability, and You do not reveal Yourself through education. Thank You, Jesus, for revealing the Father to me in ways my finite mind and soul comprehends, and *I thought I knew you then.*

April 4th, 2012

Up early to skate. Thankful for a good sleep on our second night in England.

Thank You for the "check" and reminder as I awake and began to trespass on Your sovereignty when thinking about Sandy. First, we need to seek Your wisdom and guidance because You know where this is going and at what speed. We need Your grace and love and patience! Let us not take one step or make even one decision apart from You.

And for Rich Saul, his family, Your tender mercies as his earthly life comes to its conclusion. May they experience Your presence and comfort in every step of this journey. Let them see the treasures in the midst of their sorrow that only You provide.

April 6th, 2012

Listening to the birds sing in the mountains of Canazei, Italy, after a *long* day of travel yesterday from England and a good sleep, and a one-hour skating session this a.m. Today is the "Amazing Grace" roll out on Good Friday. My "Amazing Grace" skate is scheduled around 7 p.m., and I'm the final skater in my group of 11—just where I wanted to be. Thanks Dad and thank You Father God for Jesus' grace and mercy remembering His once-and-for-all sacrifices celebrated today.

April 13th, 2012

In Paris, catching up on sleep after many long and unusual days. It was a delightful Wednesday afternoon and night in Paris with Caleb and Kylie along with Monica's girls.

Thursday's 11 hours, starting with the tour of Notre Dame Cathedral, the Shakespeare and Co. Bookstore, crepes for lunch, the Bastille area, Sacred Heart Cathedral where for over 125 years 24/7 someone has been praying. Kylie getting sketched and then dinner with piano music.

April 16th, 2012

Up very early today for 9 a.m. flight from Gatwick. A great week with Kylie. Everything went smoothly and we're on our way on schedule.

Skated Friday night for a bit of practice before Saturday's events. Pierrette and her husband Michael were so gracious, showing me a picture from last year's competition that they will use for display this weekend and thanked us for coming.

I was the only Silver IV but skated with the Silver II, felt really good and comfortable. I don't know what my score was, but at least I landed everything! At the awards, Michael gave me my trophy and another man in a hat came running out to congratulate me saying, "Just had to tell you that you had a wonderful program." Then he gave me the traditional French two-cheek kiss. Michael told me he was the chief judge and that he insisted he shake my hand. He indicated that it was a most unusual occurrence!

Sunday Silver Artistic lumped all age levels so there were five of us—I was much older than all the rest. All the other numbers were a whole lot different than "Amazing Grace." The Russian Anna went before me with "Rock Around the Clock." I had no idea how it would be received by the French, but it wasn't for them. I enjoyed myself totally, scored 33+ and placed first. All the skaters were so supportive, I was blessed! Maybe because of my age, whatever, I pray they will remember and think of Your amazing grace displayed in Jesus.

April 19th, 2012

Back home. Celebrating Your goodness and favor as all the travel skating went without a hitch, despite the short sleeps and long car and plane travel, no illness or injury.

Now I have just four short weeks before Oberstdorf. Looking forward to catching up on my time in the Word and reflecting on Your faithfulness, amazed by Your grace and mercy. So special to spend time with my youngest child and oldest grandchild as they climbed the Eiffel Tower, really? Visiting the site of the Bastille and the Sacre Coeur where someone has been praying 24/7 for 125 years!

And for Mike and Katie and the others to be able to see me skate live from Italy.

The concern I have for Sandy and lay at Your altar asking for guidance and wisdom and grace.

April 21st, 2012

I am grateful for a day like today with nothing major on my list with time to pace myself with home projects.

Thankful for Brian G. and the massage yesterday that leaves me sore but hopeful that this leg issue can be solved. Never would have thought this stage in my life I'd need the help of a body mechanic! It's rather hilarious actually, but You think of everything!

Today is the funeral for Rick Saul in Georgia. Saying good-bye is never easy, even though we know he's in Your amazing presence. Bless his family and friends as they gather to celebrate his life today. I'm trusting that the testimony of Your impact on his life and destiny will be clearly presented and cause fence-sitters to embrace Your gift of mercy and forgiveness in their lives as well.

Thank You for the gift of Today!

Psalms 89:15
Blessed are those who have learned to acclaim you, who walk in the light of your presence, O LORD.

They rejoice in your name all day long, they exult in your righteousness.

It is such a blessing to have learned to acclaim You, to give You Your rightful praise. I thank You for opening my eyes to see the wonder of Your presence. There is no place else I'd rather be. This is the very *best*, knowing You are in my life, my world, my every moment.

April 22nd, 2012

Feeling the effects still of Brian's treatment and a bit under the weather as well. Thankful I have these couple of days to rest and rebound as Mike travels to Pennsylvania and Ohio.

April 23rd, 2012

I pray for Jason's defense today. Praying humble confidence for him as he crosses the finish line!

Mike in snowy Ohio today.

Feeling better but still very congested. Thankful the timing of this is what it is, with me having days to just rest. I would have preferred to get some work done, but I am grateful for how it's developed.

Even when I'm weak, especially, I am conscious of Your solid faithfulness and strength that sustains me. I am nothing, can do nothing, apart from You.

Marsha's request to be prayed from Deuteronomy 31:8:
The Lord himself goes before you and will be with you; he will never leave you nor forsake you. Do not be afraid; do not be discouraged.

Whatever she needs to be reminded of in that, I ask your reminders to be strong and clear to her.

April 28th, 2012

Bless Sherry O. and Lisa, and all who are involved with Dribble 4 Destiny. It was such a good time in Greenville the last two days. Amazing how You use different ways to reach people: basketball skills in inner city, Chris who came to play golf and works at BMW, out of nowhere is paired with Mike.

My time at the Pavilion in Greenville. Who knew there was a skating rink there? Nice people—Kim and the one who's running the competition and Cheryl the pro who also teaches in Cumming.

April 29th, 2012

Thankful for this "still" morning with no rush, time to reflect and think. Yesterday with Lee Strobel was encouraging—to hear those who can condense the vast questions and objections people have to Jesus, and to see how much sense it makes to believe. The scientific reminders were especially encouraging. And I continue to pray for Brian and his family of scientists to see clearly the evidence that surrounds them. But ultimately each person chooses by evaluating the knowledge in their world.

I continue to thank You for making it so clear to me that You *are* who You are—absolute Truth, my Creator and Redeemer and Sustainer, and that I know that I know!

may 2012

May 4th, 2012

Thank You for Kaitlyn—twelve years old today, and Randy is thirty-one. Bless them with the reminder of Your love and the love of family and friends as they celebrate. Thank You for this quiet, stay-at-home morning where I can be still and have some time to reflect. It is raining. Mike is in Fresno. I've skated every morning this week, and my body is tired. I am still dealing with the left quad thing with just two weeks until Germany.

My conversation with Lisa on Wednesday was interesting. I am happy that my story is an encouragement to her, and I'm grateful for the blessing this return to skating has given me, to Rose, and my family. Please use it for Your glory and show me the way to honor You in the midst of it.

Just looking at the field across the street and I think of the truths
You share in Psalm 103: Your compassion as a parent, for You know
how we are formed and remember we are dust. Our days are like the
grass, flourishing like a flower in the field. The wind blows over it,
it is gone and its place remembers it no more. But, from everlasting
to everlasting, the Lord's love is with those who fear Him, and His
righteousness with their children's children.

You forgive all my sins. You heal all my diseases. You redeem my life
from the pit. You crown me with love and compassion. You satisfy my
desires with good things so that my youth is renewed like the eagle's.

Just called Kaitlyn, the happy girl. You uniquely made her and I am so
blessed—so upbeat and genuinely "happy" from the day she arrived.
Continue to shine through her, bringing joy to those around her, and
give her increasing awareness that You are her awesome God.

May 8th, 2000

What an amazing few days this has been! I thank You,
Lord, for the planning of my presence in the delivery
room when Kaitlyn was born. It was such a special
experience to see her respond to our voices. My prayer
is that she always hears Your voice behind her telling
her which way to go and that she is loved! Teach her
Your way, O Lord, and lead her in a straight path. Let
her see Your goodness in this land of the living just as
David said in Psalm 22:9-10:

You brought me out of the womb; you made me trust you
even at my mother's breast. From birth I was cast upon you;
from my mother's womb you have been my God.

This life is so new and fresh, just as Your mercies are each day. I pray for Molly and Jason as they face so many changes in the near future, that they will be so aware of the tremendous blessing this child is and that they would seek Your wisdom as they make the adjustments to changes.

My heart and my soul praise You, O My Father! I have so much to be thankful for.

May 6th, 2012

Beautiful "Super Moon" last night. There is no voice or language where Your display is not evident. The heavens declare Your glory, and I praise You for opening my eyes to it!

Yesterday, with Joy Boerup at GCC, "Does God make mistakes?" A good time with the ladies, able to catch up with Jeannie and Marsha. How I thank You for them and their friendship through the years, and to continue to hear of Your faithfulness to all of us.

So many encouraging comments about my "appearance." Yes, I've lost some weight. The skating has obviously "restored" some muscles that had been hiding for a while. My quad continues to be uncomfortable, and I'm asking for resolution to that problem soon. Talking with Jeannie and Marsha and Joy makes me realize the multi-dimensional benefits of my return to the ice—and some things I'm still becoming aware of and it's all Your goodness to me.

And yesterday as I drove to GCC and passed the truck on the highway, from Fresno, California! Now that's amazing—a coincidence, many would say. But I took it as a message from You

to pray for Mike and all the CFL (Champions For Life) teammates
going into the prisons yesterday in Fresno, California.

May 8th, 2012

Today Mike leaves for France. So glad I decided to stay home this
morning, and skate this afternoon. I do cherish my mornings in
Your Word, as You continue to speak to me—instructing, tuning,
correcting, and letting me realize that this time is not without effect!

You continue to cultivate the garden of my inner being, and You
have been so kind and gentle.

Thank You for the many times I've come to realize "that's it." When
someone says something about You and I realize that's exactly what
You've been teaching me of Yourself.

And the way You delight to do good things for Your children, and we
miss so much of it.

Thank You for yesterday's breakthrough with my quad, whatever
happened. It's been feeling so much better in answer to my request.

And thank You for Sarah doing such a good job with the beads.
I now have such a pretty dress to wear for "Amazing Grace."

Amazing God, amazing love
It's my joy to honor You.

1 Samuel 2:34, 35
You foretold this day, but promised You would raise up for yourself
a faithful priest who will do according to what is *"in my heart and
mind."* And that was Samuel.

Lord, raise up a faithful priest today who will do according to what is in Your heart and mind, I pray.

There is so much rationalization, compromise. We need witnesses for You who will stand firmly on Your Word, uncompromisingly, without shame, but being humbly dependent on You for wisdom and strength. I know there is nothing new under the sun. Don't let me be blind to the error in thoughts and actions that are not in accord with Your heart and mind.

The purposes of Your heart stand firm forever. That has never wavered and never will.

May 10th, 2012

Happy to have the opportunity to go to South Carolina today and see Katie and family.

May 13th, 2012, Mother's Day

My heart is full. Gratitude for my dear children and that each know You. For the news that grandbaby number seven is on the way and due at Christmas.

Such a sweet, brief visit with Barnetts. Spending a day with Anna Kate while everyone else did their regular Friday. Something about spending a day, deliberately with a two-year-old that is just fun! Thank You for that blessing and for her. Reading *The King of Capri* to Rody, and he really gets the story. He's so much fun to read to.

Again You have satisfied my desires with good things and my youth is renewed. And wow, how thankful I am for the improvement in my leg issue! One week ago I was still nursing great discomfort and ever since last Monday's breakthrough . . . I hated to bother You with a request. When will I learn?

1 Samuel 15:22-23
The Lord delights in obedience rather than sacrifice.

Psalm 107
Give thanks to the LORD, for he is good; his love endures forever.

Thinking about this Psalm, whatever the situation, when they cried out to You, You listened and acted. You led them by a straight way and brought them out of darkness and deepest gloom. You sent forth Your word and healed them. You stilled the storm to a whisper and guided them to their desired haven.

The upright see and rejoice!

May 14th, 2007

The celebration of Mother's Day is less painful as the years go, knowing that You in Your sovereignty designed my mother for me. You also gave me her mother Gladys and her mother Rose Secoy Moore in my heritage! And You have allowed me to look into the window of their souls and to see Your faithfulness through the generations.

You guided Rose (Secoy Moore) and Gladys to their desired haven with You.

May 2ⁿᵈ, 2004

From Roxboro, I pray today and thank You for the wonderful reminders of Your faithfulness as I spend time with my children and grandchildren.

Psalm 102
Regardless of my circumstances, *You Lord, sit enthroned forever; Your renown endures through all generations. You remain the same, and your years will never end.*

I know they will thrive in Your presence. I can only imagine Rose Secoy Moore as she faced her earthly death, praying for future generations to thrive in Your presence. Thank You for remembering Your promise to her, that I see the day when her Redeemer lives—not only in me, but in my children, her great-great-grandchildren.

May 28ᵗʰ, 2009

I think of how You ordained for me to be in Wisconsin and get to know my Grandma Gladys, to have the joy, which has increased over the years, to hear her say through her tears, with such gratitude: "You have reintroduced me to an old friend." If nothing else to get to know my great-grandmother as a result, to hold her Bible in my hand, truly a gift from You!

As Proverbs 14:10 says *no one else can fully share my joy.* It is a unique gift from You to me, from You to Gladys— I'm sure as an assured mother's prayer. I see clearly Your love demonstrated to Gladys long after her mother's dying prayer was prayed. You took care of her child and reminded her of You in her final years.

May 17th, 2012

Today I leave for Germany—the International Adult Figure Skating Competitions. Seems unreal that I would be doing this. You do indeed satisfy my desires with good things so that youth are renewed.

Let Your light shine through me, may the words of my mouth be pleasing in Your sight. May the message of "Amazing Grace" capture the attention of hearts who are not yet devoted to You.

All this is evidence of Your goodness, let Your light shine so the whole world sees, I pray.

Okay. Jesus moment. You knew, You ordained that after my heart prayed, today's reading would be John 9, so my tears of amazement flow. You did this just for me, from all eternity You knew this day would be as it is—my earthly daddy's favorite hymn. I am a skating 63-year-old grandmother traveling the world with my little sister in honor of our dad's memory. How I heard the Celtic Woman "Amazing Grace" at the ice rink and immediately said, "I want to skate to this." Davin cutting the part he did, "It means different things to different people."

Lisa helping with the choreography, loving the program, and connecting with the music and words every time. Today praying the message will speak.

And then I come to John 9. Jesus heals the man born blind. For heaven's sake, You are absolutely amazing!

The purpose of this blind man's condition according to Jesus: *"This happened so that the works of God might be displayed in his life." "I am the light of the world."*

Lord, I believe and I worship You, and I praise You for giving me this opportunity on this stage to declare Your message!

I could not have imagined a better, more personal, send off. Here I go in Your amazing grace and surrounded by Your favor.

Psalm 147:11
The Lord delights in those who fear him, who put their hope in his unfailing love.

May 21st, 2012

Day three in Oberstorf, and the sun is shining again and the view of the mountains from our balcony is spectacular. You continue to tread the high places of the earth and reveal Your thoughts to man.

I'm grateful for this morning and the opportunity to be still in my soul and activity. It has been a little more challenging to adjust to the time and maybe altitude this year, so having a few days to ease into it is such a blessing.

Psalm 116:7-9
Be at rest once more, O my soul, for the LORD has been good to you. For you, O LORD, have delivered my soul from death, my eyes from

tears, my feet from stumbling, that I may walk before the LORD *in the land of the living.*

My soul is at rest. Let my ambitions find rest as well that I may find my delight in You alone.

May 22ⁿᵈ, 2012

Another beautiful morning in the mountains of Germany.

Amos 4:13
He who forms the mountains, creates the wind, and reveals his thoughts to man, he who turns dawn to darkness, and treads the high places of the earth—the LORD *God Almighty is his name.*

So much *visible* evidence of You in this place! So sweet to meet Carinne Stewart from Vancouver yesterday, and her husband Don, celebrating 35 years.

May 23ʳᵈ, 2012

My artistic skate event is this morning at 10—the first event of the competition. And I skate third of five. I am excited! It is my joy to honor You. I worship You, Lord. Let my performance be a tribute to You, I ask. You are my audience!

And Monica skates right after me—"Over the Rainbow," good for a rainy day. You still the storms to a whisper, and send rainbows as a reminder. Thank You for this day!

Back to the apartment for a little rest. My skate was so special—just
a joy! And the judges awarded me first place, but You were my only
audience that mattered! And it brought Monica to tears.

Monica skated beautifully and would have placed 2nd, but she had
a time deduction. She was happy with her marks and placed 4th.
But it's all good. We are here and thankful for You and Your
goodness to us.

May 24th, 2012

Magnificent storm last night with lighting over the mountains—
such fun to watch. I'm thankful today, a day off to just rest and
enjoy. Good thing we left the Awards Ceremony as soon as we
got ours so we were able to beat most of the rain, thunder,
and lighting.

May 25th, 2012

Up at 6 a.m. for our 15-minute skate at 7 a.m. Beautiful,
cool morning. So grateful for this day surrounded by the
mountains You formed and Your favor. And being able to be here,
and participate in something I enjoy—that is truly a gift from You!

Absolutely amazing grace, so underserved. I realize that most of
those I learned to skate with are not able to do this for various
reasons, yet You have allowed me to, and with joy! I pray that
I will be a witness of this to my fellow competitors and the
audience. If Dad can see from his place of eternal rest, I know
he will be proudly smiling and that is a delight. But I know that
You are.

Psalm 33:13-14

From heaven the LORD *looks down and sees all mankind; from his dwelling place he watches all who live on earth.*

Another Jesus moment as I read today's scriptures. Starting with 2 Samuel 7, and I knew right away and it brought tears.

David's desire to build something for You after he was settled in his palace and experienced rest from his enemies. And Your message to him through Nathan.

You brought them to this place, and Your plans are better than anything we can imagine. You establish legacies. You are in control.

Then David sat before You.

2 Samuel 7:18

Who am I, O Sovereign LORD, *and what is my family, that you have brought me this far?*

I remember meditating on that at Katie and Randy's wedding. And now thinking how Dad told me four-and-a-half years before he died that this was not how he thought things would be. Is it ever? With You in control, I can know that it is as You planned and, good or bad, compared to what we imagined—You've got it. You can be trusted to be faithful.

And Mike and I having 42 years together at this point, and where we are and how You've blessed us so much more than I ever could have planned.

Psalm 119:35-37

Direct me in the path of your commands, for there I find delight. Turn

my heart toward your statutes and not toward selfish gain. Turn my eyes
away from worthless things; preserve my life according to your word.

You have been faithful to direct me in the path of Your commands
and, in my heart, I can say I have all I ever could have wanted.
There is nothing I lack because I have You!

The most important thing to You is to be a "man after my own
heart"—to desire the things that are important to You brings You
the most delight. And in turn our delight is to honor You!

May 26th, 2012

Another beautiful morning in Bavaria. Yesterday, I skated third of
six. Not my best, but placed 2nd and I was just thrilled to be able to
do it. Then I rented a bike and peddled for over an hour through
the countryside along the river. It was spectacular. After wardrobe
consultation with Monica, I returned to the rink for a few hours
before the awards. I didn't get back to the apartment until almost
midnight, completely spent! 4 ½ miles walking and then the bik-
ing and skating—oh my!

But all with a heart of gratitude! My sincere thankfulness for all
You have allowed me to do.

May 27th, 2012

From Munich airport hotel awaiting return home in the morning.
Yesterday, was "hilarious" as Monica won the Gold II freestyle. She
did so well! And I know she was thrilled. It was a long day with
packing, the awards ceremony, banquet, and a celebration—we
didn't get to bed until 1:20 a.m.! Monica's 56th birthday.

Talked with a male skater from Italy. Said he skated with Victoria and saw me skate in Canazei, and, "many times on YouTube." It made me laugh. Now I just catch up on my reading and get a good sleep.

This has been such a special nine days for Monica and me. Time together, and time apart. A lovely place, time to talk of life and blessings, survival, and Your faithfulness with both of us being at the place of trust in Your sovereignty . . .

Monica the Chaplain, coming to the aid of Eileen, Liz, Elena the Russian, and being able to bless others with her gifts of encouragement. My friends the Fins, Sirkha and Helena, so much fun. Victoria the Italian, Lupita from Mexico, and Tatiana from Moscow. It was good to meet Julie and Liz from California, and Maggie Harding the personal trainer from San Francisco. And of course Carinne Stewart from Vancouver, and Adele from Australia via Northern Ireland who skated to Celtic Woman's "Amazing Grace," and how her daughters helped her choose the music. Her dad was a Baptist minister!

May 29th, 2012

Back safely in my "happy room" with a heart full of special memories from my time with Monica in Germany and from the many interactions with our new friends from all over the world. I would/ could have never imagined having such an experience and knowing that You had this all planned is beyond gratitude! You delight to do good things for Your children and I have so much proof.

2 Samuel 14:14
Like water spilled on the ground, which cannot be recovered, so we must die. But God does not take away life; instead, he devises ways so that a banished person may not remain estranged from him.

For some reason this verse has always struck me, words from a "wise woman" to the king—through her David came to see that he was treating Absalom in a manner "not after God's heart."

You do, Lord, desire to restore those who are banished from their closeness to You, and You provide ways for that restoration. Each person needs to come to You for that, their choice.

Psalm 119:111-112
Your statutes are my heritage forever; they are the joy of my heart. My heart is set on keeping your decrees to the very end.

Proverbs 16:9
In his heart a man plans his course, but the LORD determines his steps.

May 30th, 2012

Enjoying another early morning as I adjust to the jet lag. Mike off to Boston University for tests. Many different concerns on my heart today, over missionary families around the world, but I know that You have your eye and hand on each.

No matter what my burden or concern, knowing that You've got it covered and are aware and working gives me such rest. Thank You for faithfully teaching me according to Your Word and reminding me whenever I tend to worry!

May 31st, 2012

Thank You for Your faithful protection over Mike as he participates in this medical study in Boston.

I had a long talk with Caleb yesterday. Give him guidance and clear direction as he nears a decision about graduate school. You know the plans You have for him. He's come so far in his faith, and my request is that You clearly direct him on the path that will keep his heart gripped to You.

I'm grateful for this day. Skating yesterday was good, but I realize my body needs some rest from this training. Help me make wise decisions and to use this gift of time in June to be refreshed and focused on the year ahead.

Still so grateful for the nine days in Oberstdorf. Such a restful place, away from the way life is. Time with Monica and being able to skate, such a sweet gift from You, and I never would have imagined or could have planned it. Yet from Your abundant goodness, You provided it. I'm so grateful that You did and that You let me see your provision was from You.

I think back to 1996, when my parents moved to Georgia, and all that I've been through since then. And to be at this place now where the fruit of me, my lot has fallen in pleasant places for sure.

june 2012

June 1st, 2012

The month of "rest" begins. Thank You for getting Mike home safely last night; even though they couldn't do the spinal tap, at least they got data that will be useful in their medical study.

Psalm 119:37
Turn my eyes away from worthless things; preserve my life according to your word.

My goal and eyes aren't on earthly prizes but on You, for there I find delight.

Wisdom is much more valuable than man's honor. To be known as Your humble child seeking to honor You in all I do is my only goal. What place I receive in a skating competition is not important.

June 2nd, 2012

At some point in Germany I was thinking of John 21—the dialogue between Peter and Jesus. But I couldn't remember the address. Today here it is, and now I can't remember why I was thinking about it, but . . .

Jesus, You have prepared works for me to do. You know my heart and know it all. You continue to direct my steps and empower me for every situation. Everything has a purpose; it's all part of Your sovereign plan. If I love You, I will do as You command. The times You asked Peter, "Do you love me?" You asked three times, not because he didn't hear You each time, or that You didn't hear him.

Your command is always "Follow me." That is how we glorify God. The desire You have for me is to "follow me."

That's it. Not to be concerned about others whatever near or far—just to do what You have prepared for me where You have placed me. Not to be jealous or proud, just focused.

Proverbs 16:16
How much better to get wisdom than gold, to choose understanding rather than silver!

June 5th, 2012

Day five of rest. It is so pleasant to spend day after day in an unhurried pace, not that there is not much to do, it's just not hectic. The moments come—like yesterday's stockholders meeting and that extra time on the phone with Delta getting Las Vegas seats secured. So, we're going to Las Vegas with Monte and Phyllis and other Raiders to commemorate the life of the now-deceased owner, Al Davis.

Great news that Baby Barnett is doing well and scheduled to arrive December 21st.

I ask for rest for Katie from the stress of this season of her life. Give her joy in this journey.

June 6th, 2012

Yesterday, I skated—fun—and felt good during all my jumps and spins. The little boy from the summer camp was so funny—talk about saying, "What's on your mind?"! Kids are so funny.

Still enjoying camping in Psalm 33.
In him our hearts rejoice, for we trust in his holy name.

Acts 4:29
Now, Lord, consider their threats and enable your servants to speak your word with great boldness.

For all the believers in hard places I pray Your courage, protection, and rest in Your unfailing love as they carry on.

June 7th, 2012

Oh what a beautiful morning. Cool and sunny, and the birds chirp-
ing delightfully. Makes it seem like all is as it should be. Even though
I know it's not, at least for this brief time as I sit with You and
contemplate Your Word, refreshment comes and just a hint of what
it will be someday when everything truly is as it should be. Oh, how I
look forward to that day. And in the meantime, You continue to be the
faithful Father I have come to know and trust.

Give Molly peace and confidence as she takes her boards today. Thank
You for the gift of time at the beach so unexpected—looks like Kylie,
Karson, Katie, and her two will be coming. You are so good!

July 9th, 2009

The sun is shining, the candle lit—sitting in my "Happy
Room" surrounded by "stuff" that connects me to
my heritage. Grandma Gladys's dresser and lamps,
handmade things by the Szparaga family, Caleb's
first (and only) cowboy boots, a gift from Ken and
Shirley Snelling, pictures of children and grandchildren,
many earthly treasures, and Your Word, my daily bread,
for which I am eternally grateful. It tells me of Your
mercy which triumphs over judgment, Your faithfulness
despite my feelings, and Your compassion that meets
every need.

June 9th, 2012

This has been just a restful week with signs of Your goodness unfolding every day. Thank You for each blessing.

Mission trips. Kylie and Jason going to Ethiopia next month and now dealing with the changes in their team. I know You're teaching Kylie through all this that man makes his plans but You direct his steps.

Dave Straughan's heart issues just yesterday that will probably thwart his plans to go to Spain next week. Make Your Will known, and give Dave and Kathy assurance You've got it all under control.

June 11th, 2012

I love Solomon's prayer in 1 Kings 8. It covered all the bases and concludes with, *"And may these words of mine, which I have prayed before the LORD be near to the LORD our God day and night, that he may uphold the cause of his servant . . . according to each day's need."*

You know the concerns of his heart as he so clearly prayed, but he realized each day's need in the future would be different, and he was expressing his plan that You would hold his requests near night and day, and You would act according to the need of the moment.

I like that, because even though I should pray without ceasing, You have got Your eyes on the situation and You're watching from heaven, and I can trust You to hold my heart's concerns near and act according to each day's need. Thank You.

June 13th, 2012

How Solomon went from 1 Kings 8 to 1 Kings 11—700 wives, 300 concubines and to doing evil in Your eyes, his heart turned away from You. He had everything; Godly heritage, success, possession, and education, but he did not guard his heart and as a result he left a legacy of unfaithfulness. How very sad!

June 14th, 2012

How can it be Thursday already? Nice time with some GCC ladies last night. Today I have an MRI for that lump in my quad. Trusting Your unfailing love for my benefit.

I enjoyed reading my journal from 2007-2008. Some great memories and reminders of Your goodness in the midst of it all.

India Brooks is on my heart as she fights her battle physically and emotionally. Give her strength for each need as only You can. Remind her that even in her pain, You are with her, every breath, and give her family and care team wisdom to make the best decisions for her.

June 19th, 2012

From Fripp Island. Bless Mike and Mary for their kindness to us. Arrived Sunday for a week with Katie, Rody, Anna Kate, Kylie, and Karson. Such a beautiful place where Your creation is on display. After two times asking Anna Kate, "Who made the ocean?" and her answers being, "Mommy, Daddy, Grandma, etc.," she finally said "Jesus!" Yeah! Yes indeed, and not only did You make it, You gather the waters of the sea into jars and put the deep into storehouses.

MRI results show a 7x7x5cm hemorrhage, or something. So I need to see an orthopedic specialist to resolve.

Thank You for Your amazing goodness.

June 24th, 2012

Back home. Exhausted from activity and hours in the car, but a good sleep and a thankful heart is the best medicine!

Something about the ocean side and the view of the heavens—all clear reminders of Your glory displayed that refreshes my soul. And again I am so grateful for this gift, and again I ask Your blessing on Mike and Mary for their kindness to us.

June 26th, 2012

Quite a long and exhausting day yesterday. Now facing a biopsy on my quad as it continues to bother me. MRI and visit with Brad Register and now referral to Emory. Lord, I trust You to work this for good. Calm any anxious thought and delight my soul with Your Word and promises. I cherish Your faithfulness and trust Your loving kindness.

Oh, the reminders yesterday of Rose's age, repetition, and slowness.

Lots to do today. I do need Your guidance to pace myself and not get distracted. I'm so grateful for Your provision, even for the many things I'm not aware of.

June 27th, 2012

Hopefully I'll know something definitive today regarding my quad—it's the not knowing that is the hardest. Pretty uncomfortable all day yesterday due to swelling. Ugh!

Caleb has a torn tendon in his thumb so hopefully the Grenoble team will make sure that gets fixed soon. Thank You for protecting him through the season from injury.

Knowing that from Your dwelling place You watch all who live on the earth, knowing that You see it all, gives me great comfort and assurance. That You will always have my back, and You will fulfill Your purpose for me in Your amazing ways!

June 28th, 2012

Praising You for the new mercies You faithfully provide each day. I'm so glad yesterday is over, and the biopsy is done. Now I'll wait and trust Your provision and protection as I face the next—and hopefully last step—to get this resolved.

Thank You that I can trust You knowing my welfare is in Your hands. My loving and compassionate Father.

June 29th, 2012

Thankful that I was able to walk two miles yesterday. And I'm increasingly aware of Your kindness that allowed me to be physically able to go to Germany and skate just one month ago. You had to have intervened because there is no way I could have competed or even

made the trip in my current state. How I praise You for Your goodness that mercifully held these symptoms at bay, suspended
reality by the touch of Your hand, just so Monica and I could have
that time together. And to think I was able to travel, walk the streets
of Oberstdorf, practice and compete in both events without
feeling the restrictions of the ailment! You didn't have to intervene
in this way, but You did, and I see it clearly now. You are able and
You delight to do good things for Your children. Thank You for
doing this for me, and for allowing me to see and understand how
You did something special just for me.

My heart is heavy for Angie Bundy as she continues to battle
severe headaches. Give her a sign of Your goodness today that she
may see clearly Your provision.

Okay, another wonderful Jesus moment. As I got my second cup
of coffee and shared the previous thought with Mike as I hobbled
up the stairs and I sat down in my chair, the Word of Psalm 147
came to mind.

- *Sing to the LORD with thanksgiving.*
- *The LORD sustains the humble.*
- *Great is our God and mighty in power; his understanding has no limit.*
- *His pleasure is not in the strength of the horse, nor his delight in the legs of a man.*
- *The LORD delights in those who fear Him, who put their hope in his unfailing love.*

And then I remembered since I read Psalm 146 yesterday, Psalm
147 would be today's reading . . . sob! So, I just re-read May
17th. The day I left for Germany, how I concluded with words
from Psalm 147. And then the personal Jesus moment on May 25th.

Things never are what we imagine or maybe even plan. Your plans for us are so much more amazing than we could ever plan.

Thank You again for the delightful reminders that You surround me with favor as with a shield. The longing of my heart is to honor You and You proved in ways that speak to me personally that You are my faithful Father!

June 30th, 2012

Last day of the month—our planned month of rest! I guess we did but not always in ways we planned. My leg slowly is returning to normal size, but anticipating the next procedure, I ask Your calm for my anxieties. It's not that I don't trust You to take care of everything but I'm concerned about the timing and recovery as we leave in 21 days for three weeks in Pennsylvania.

Fun to read my travel journals from 2007-08. England trip with Esther, Germany at Christmas and all the Euros! Then Camp of the Peaks in June, Poland in July, more Euros from Lufthansa, and return. That was five years ago. Life goes on and Your faithfulness and provision is amazing.

Buying a new van which will allow me to keep my leg elevated on our trip, and now being able to provide Katie and Randy with a good used van they've been praying about—only You can do these unexpected things. And through it all, blessings to so many.

july 2012

July 2nd, 2012

Message yesterday was from Romans 9—such a good reminder. Paul had such a deep love for the Jewish people and had such a burden for them to "see" as he had come to see and understand, to the point of being willing to sacrifice himself for their sake. And Paul's respect for his people—their rich history and unique blessing—yet they did not believe, receive the Messiah sent by You of whom the Scriptures spoke.

Good to spend time with Ann and George yesterday. She appears to be a great asset to him. You use everything we have in our experience to teach us and train us and mold us. I pray You help them finish strong in the years left to them. Bless them as they seek to serve You with the gifts You've given them.

Tomorrow to Vegas, help me to use today to accomplish productive results I ask. This quad has been such a thorn with this wearisome discomfort and restricted movement. That this surgery can get scheduled and I can begin to return to normal. I know You've got me held tight but, just reminding You that I'm trusting You to be faithful.

July 3rd, 2012

Thank You, Lord, for the gift of Molly—amazing 39 years! Bless her today as she celebrates with her family, that she would grasp the thought and depth and width of Your love for her as she reflects on her years. What an amazing creation!

You alone know how she is wired. So in those places where she needs comfort, be her comfort and her rest. Give her assurance that You are pleased with her. Wrap Your loving arms around her in a way that speaks to her deepest needs. My prayer is that she will never have a day when she doubts Your love for her and that she will always walk in confidence that You are directing her steps. Give her eyes to see Your favor surrounding her—that she may grow in her knowledge and understanding of You.

Dreamed last night about pain. Praying Your solution for my leg, and asking Your mercy in Angie as she continues to battle her headaches.

Now, off to Vegas! Curious to see why You added this surprise to our calendar?

July 4th, 2012

Slept until nine in the morning Vegas time—that would be noon at home. Travel yesterday must have been tiring. Enjoying a quiet morning before more Raiders events this afternoon and evening. Amazing how so many lives were brought together through Al Davis, as we're here as his guests to honor his memory.

In this place—the gambling, the immorality, supposedly built by the mob—I pray for people who are here for this event! As we walk through and among the thousands who are here for ungodly purposes, certainly not a place I would have ever chosen to come. As You look from heaven on this place in the desert, what but infinite mercy. How it must grieve Your heart to see people You created seek satisfaction in such senseless ways! I ask You to open my eyes and heart to see what You want me to see and give me words of wisdom to speak and ask those You put in my path what pleases You.

As I sit here and process the sights of what man and his wealth have built that robs so many of what You desire for them, it makes my heart hurt. Have mercy, Lord Jesus.

July 6th, 2012

Back home, still waiting for info on my quad. Please Lord, I'm weary from this ongoing situation and I'm so ready to get it resolved. You know the timetable—I'm trusting You. I'm just expressing my weary heart because I know You understand.

So long, Vegas. My oh my—wonderful to connect with so many old acquaintances and to meet new ones. I pray for all the "girlfriends"

I met and had conversations with. May something I said remain with each lady if it benefits their journey to You. Otherwise, let them forget everything I contributed.

I pray also for whomever that guy is who has such fond memories of eating dinner at our house when he was a rookie.

It's all so sad and real and heart-wrenching that man continues to reject Jesus and not do what is right and just do whatever he wants.

Lord, have mercy!

July 7th, 2012

Think of those who today celebrate their five-year wedding anniversaries, 7-7-7. How many are thriving?

What a treat to see You bless Katie and Randy by providing our old van for them! You provided for us and then the blessing continued. Thank You for these sweet hugs from Rody and Anna Kate yesterday—such a gift!

Now the news that I have a malignancy in my leg is not what I expected to hear. And so the journey begins of consults, tests, plans. But as I drove to South Carolina yesterday in the quiet, all I could think was to praise You, that I know You are sovereign over my life and death and welfare, and that whatever the future holds, I know You've got me firmly in Your grasp! I am at peace.

I ask that You help us to just rest in Your care, give the doctors wisdom beyond their ability. So many plans have been made and now it's all on hold as we wait to hear the details.

As I walked to the mailbox this morning and breathed in the fresh air, I am aware of how healthy I feel apart from my quad. So, I am thankful for that blessing.

Psalm 5:1-3

Give ear to my words, O LORD consider my sighing.

Listen to my cry for help,

my King and my God,

For to you I pray.

In the morning, O LORD, you hear my voice; in the morning I lay my requests before you and wait in expectation.

Psalm 5:11-12

Let all who take refuge in you be glad; let them ever sing for joy.

Spread your protection over them, that those who love your name may rejoice in you.

For surely, O LORD, you bless the righteous; you surround them with your favor as with a shield.

I do love these words—Your Word—and that You knew that this was part of today's reading. Sweet reminders!

July 9th, 2012

Words from Psalm 103 come to mind this morning as I begin my quiet time. I am praising You, Lord—all that is within me—and trying not to forget all Your benefits. You forgive all, You heal all. You redeem and crown with love and compassion. You satisfy and renew strength.

From everlasting to everlasting Your love is with those who fear You, and Your righteousness with their children's children.

Today we shall get a clearer picture from the doctor of just what I am facing. I feel like my emotions have been suspended for a few days, knowing this diagnosis but not really understanding what it means.

It's true that I can't know the future, but I know beyond a doubt that You hold the future. My heart's desire is that You be honored and glorified in my life. You have been so merciful and kind throughout my life, and I'm just so very grateful to be at this place where when I received the news that was not expected, my first inclination was to praise You. I have learned, as You have been my faithful Teacher, that You are sovereign in the most loving and tender and personal ways. Amazing grace indeed.

The request that I lay before You is that You give us clear heads and discerning wisdom to process the details and to chart the best course for this battle. Every case is different said Julie Brown, but You are the only wise God in whom I place my trust.

Also, I ask these things for Zoe Roberts as she just received news of her cancer and meets with professionals tomorrow for a strategy meeting. Give her a good, joyful day today and many reminders of Your loving care.

July 10th, 2012

Today, I awake to find myself refreshed, so thankful for sleep! Yesterday was hard—first drive to the hospital for a consult with the doctor, Radiology Oncologist. Again the news was not what I expected as the course of treatment is five weeks of radiation, a few weeks recovery, and then surgery to remove the sarcoma. We had lots of questions, a lot to think about—and knowing I had to let the kids know this much. Molly called as we were leaving the hospital so it was easy to just be honest, and so good that she understands. Then trying to compose a concise email, and Monica's phone call. Thank You for her!

It was hard meeting with Wayne and Carmen for dinner and avoiding the subject while consoling them after each has lost a dear family member in the last month.

Tomorrow, I have the scans so that will complete the information, and then we can proceed. I'm just so ready to get going and fight this battle.

This morning I am comforted by:

Psalm 112:1-2, 7
Blessed is the man who fears the LORD, *who finds great delight in his commands. His children will be mighty in the land; the generations of the upright will be blessed. . . . He will have no fear of bad news; his heart is steadfast, trusting in the* LORD.

And this explains my condition at this moment. I am so blessed finding delight in Your Word, and having no fear of bad news, just trusting You, because I know.

You work everything together for good for me to conform me into the image of Jesus, and You will fulfill Your purpose for me, among so much else.

And I am experiencing Your peace that defies understanding. I ask that You help me to stay focused on You, the only sovereign One, who delights to do good things for His children.

This is the day You have made, I will rejoice and be glad in it!

July 11th, 2012

Off for scans today. Gathering more information to see if there is anything else going on.

The consult with the doctor yesterday was interesting and almost overwhelming. Her admiration to find ways to de-stress I'm sure came from a good heart, but I honestly feel like I am resting in You and Your faithfulness. Sure my mind goes to places of "what ifs," but I'm not staying there. I'm not falling apart emotionally. I just want to know what's going on and what my options for battle are.

So, another day in this new season. I'm counting on Your presence to calm any anxieties and to carry me safely through. You are my ever-faithful God.

Oh, and just for the record, I appreciate the sweet reminder that did bring a tear to my eye Monday night as we were driving to dinner. The car that passed us with the plates "DPS" (David Paul Spalding). Thank You for my daddy and all the wonderful memories I have of time with him.

Bless Mike as he goes to Virginia today. Give him rest from his stress and enjoyment by being with Molly and her boys!

Psalm 9:9-10
The LORD is a refuge for the oppressed, a stronghold in times of trouble. Those who know your name will trust in you, for you, LORD, have never forsaken those who seek you.

July 12ᵗʰ, 2001

Lord, this has been an incredible week. I don't know if I'm just getting old or if there is just too much on my plate. I am spent. I come to You again this morning, longing for You and Your sweet embrace. I know You are my hiding place. You give me songs of deliverance!

July 13ᵗʰ, 2012

Yesterday, was an early morning drive for a 9 a.m. appointment with the oncologist. I liked her direct approach. Good news that my bone scan was fine—my abdomen and organs too. Just five tiny lung spots that are not a great concern to her, and truthfully, any chemo would give only a ten percent chance of effectiveness. So it looks like I'll proceed with the radiation and nutritional approach.

I'm grateful for the couple of days for some soul time. So much info and so much to consider, then having to talk through it with family, so really not much down time.

I enjoyed reading Randy Dodd's book yesterday. As I was waiting in the examination room, I read the chapter about his chaplain mentor being diagnosed with inoperable and extensive cancer. Talk about timing, but it certainly could have been Your timing.

It's been one week since I received the unexpected news. Not really much time to digest and process, but I'm trusting You to give my soul rest from anxiety as You remind me of Your faithfulness, to me and all who delight themselves in You. You have been so much fun, if only we would consistently take You at Your Word. But of course we have to know Your Word to apply it, I'm so grateful for all You have taught me.

1 Chronicles 16:8-11

Give thanks to the LORD, *call on his name; make known among the nations what he has done. Sing to him, sing praise to him; tell of all his wonderful acts. Glory in his holy name; let the hearts of those who seek the* LORD *rejoice.*
Look to the LORD *and his strength; seek his face always.*

Keep Kylie and Jason in Your care. Bless them and their team as they minster in Ethiopia. Thank You for all You're letting them see, and give them energy to be a blessing to all who cross their paths these next two weeks for Your glory.

July 14th, 2012

The words of 1 Chronicles 17 are so similar to 2 Samuel 7. It's always a blessing to see David's humble heart.

This past week has been full of consults and tests and emotions. It's been overwhelming at times, but each day, each hour, I try to concentrate on staying in the moment, not able to request anything except the peace of Your presence. And You have been faithful to hold me tight, and of course, I ask for wisdom and clear thinking as we proceed.

Plans have been made to line up the radiation treatments to begin on July 23rd. It looks like Maggie will be able to be with me for the first one. Help me to think clearly of questions that need to be asked so I have the clearest possible picture of what to expect. Then Monday, I consult with a nutritionist. Preparing for that is quite taxing as she's requested lots of info.

Thanks for yesterday, and a "new" normal kind of day started with a walk, errands to Jefferson, Skyping with Monica and then Katie, and vacuuming. Never got to my sewing projects, but that's okay. Met today with Mother for a bit—mercy, mercy—and a trip to the natural food store in Athens.

Romans 2:4 is in reference to judging others, and how subtly these judgments enter my mind. Forgive me, Lord! Showing contempt for Your kindness, tolerance, and patience in what is reflected when I begin to judge, and You put it so straightforward. How did I ever miss this?!

July 15th, 2012

To GCC this morning. Feeling good, strong. Was able to talk with Peggy Ferrante yesterday—the first non-family member who I was able to have a normal conversation with since this news. Thank You, Lord, for her. Bless her as she prepares for her Nepal trip. I was hoping to be a part of her team, so maybe there is still somehow I can.

Lord, there is nothing too difficult for You. Certainly not my health situation—it's a minor issue over which You have complete authority. I ask that You keep your protective eye upon me and help me to process all the info that they are bombarding us with so that the wisest decisions will be made. Man has opinions, based on education, but You made my body and only You know how I am wired and connected; and what is best.

July 16th, 2012

Here I am at the start of another week. Taking time to place my life in Your hands figuratively, because I know I'm already safely there, acknowledging Your sovereignty and resting in assurance of Your continued faithfulness. Where would I be apart from You?

Time at GCC was dear to me yesterday as it was good to see and hug dear friends, and to be prayed for by family who surrounded me with their love and compassion. Thank You for that gift!

Tim and Cindy Sullivan suggesting I get an opinion from MD Anderson in Houston, that has already been put into motion.

So, forward with this sweet, special time in Your Word where I can be encouraged, refreshed, trained for battle, and reminded of what You have taught me of Yourself—that You are able to do exceedingly and abundantly more than I ask or imagine. Thank You for this opportunity to learn a new dimension of Your amazing grace.

And my plea for Esther and her family is that You help them to continue to focus on what is true, and to have physical, emotional, and spiritual strength to act in ways that honor You. May the words of their mouths and meditations of their hearts be pleasing to You and may no root of bitterness grow, love covers a multitude, and nothing is beyond Your redemptive hand.

Romans 3:21-22
Now a righteousness from God, apart from law, has been made known, to which the law and the Prophets testify. This righteousness from God comes through faith in Jesus Christ to all who believe.

July 17th, 2012

In my heart I am standing firm before You to thank and praise You. You are worthy of all praise!

What can I say about yesterday? It was overwhelming to say the least. Started with the radiation treatment set up, questions answered. So ready to get started on blasting this cancer.

Then a phone consult with Brenda. She's knowledgeable, but basically every food choice I make appears to contribute to cancer. And then the emotional part—questions about my mother. Somehow we never get away from the impact of the mother, do we? Certainly she has added much stress to my life, but I honestly feel You've helped me so much in that area, accepting that I can't change her, but knowing You've placed her here in my world for me to serve her in her last years.

Good, brief chat with Monica.

My evening pleas—just give me wisdom, help me to sort the counsel of the varied opinions. Help me to make the best choices. Exhausting day, to bed early—thankful sleep comes easily.

Today we meet with Dr. Dave, asking for his input. Give him Your wisdom as he listens to our dilemma that his voice can be a wise counselor for us.

Psalm 13:6
I will sing to the LORD, for he has been good to me.

I know that You have been good to me, and I trust in Your unfailing love and goodness. Onward, keep my heart at rest as I trust in You.

July 17ᵗʰ, 2002

An early morning walk to beat the heat ended with the sighting of a deer running down our street. It brought

a smile to my heart as I thought of Jason's excitement
of seeing a deer cross the path over Caleb last year at
Camp Fitch. You planned that special moment just
for me, Lord. How I praise You for the ways You show
Your goodness to me! Then reading in Isaiah 41:20, I
see how You promise to put created things in places we
normally wouldn't expect to see them, *so that people
may see and know, may consider and understand, that
the hand of the LORD has done this; that the Holy one of
Israel has created it.* There is no other explanation. You
are God and have done great and mighty things and this
day has reminded me afresh how personal You are.

July 18th, 2012

Waking up before 6 a.m. Thank You for that, so I could be lifting
Caleb to You as he's having his thumb surgery. Confident that You've
got him wrapped in Your protective shield as You give the medical
people wisdom. And for the Ethiopia team as they battle weather
and some physical discomforts. I know that You will protect and
fulfill Your purpose for them and their mission. I pray they not miss
a single awareness of Your tender mercies and personal kindness in
the midst of their service.

Thank You for Dr. Dave, for his faith in You and his willingness to
listen and be objective. I still have that sweet memory of meeting
him almost twelve years ago when he was on my dad's case post-
stroke at Gwinnett Medical. As we discussed the feeding tube
issue he asked, "How's he doing spiritually?" He knows if someone
is ready to meet You extraordinary measures to keep them here are
cruel. And even so, You had over four more years for my daddy to
live, so Your plans stand firm. You know the number of days planned

for each of us before even one of them is lived. You have always known and will continue to know.

Romans 5:1-5 gives me perfect encouragement for today.

Your peace through Jesus gives me access to the grace in which I now stand, rejoicing in the hope of the glory of God.

July 19th, 2012

Happy 68th birthday to Sandy. Bless her with a fun day and lots of reminders of Your blessing in her life.

Another day yesterday of so much more to think about, and I'm really grateful for Becky Black's thoughts. The temptation is to put faith in a program or a treatment when our only real hope is in You. It's that matter of stewardship—use of the provisions and talents You've given meant to make God-honoring choices in this. My desire is to honor You, and I know You are in control.

I do hate that I can't be with my sweet family at Fitch this year. Such a fun time as they prepare to gather, counting the days. I know You've prepared fun and memory-making times for them. Thank You.

Continue to heal Caleb, from his surgery, and thank You for surrounding him in all of the details yesterday. Great news from Ethiopia about the response of those 19 children to the Gospel. Without the confidence that You are that team's Shield and Protector, I'd tend to worry. Dear 14-year-old Kylie, help her to see You at work in ways she will be encouraged by, and help her as she readjusts her worldview through this time.

1 Chronicles 28:9-10

Acknowledge the God of your father, and serve him with wholehearted devotion and a willing mind, for the LORD searches every heart and understands every motive behind the thoughts. If you seek him, he will be found by you.

July 20th, 2012

Thank You, Lord, that You are unchangeable, and You are faithful.

Proverbs 19:21

Many are the plans of a man's heart, but it is the LORD's purpose that prevails.

But the previous verse says: *Listen to advice and accept instruction, and in the end you will be wise.*

For two weeks now we've been listening to all kinds of advice, and just when I think a plan has been decided upon, more advice flies in the window for us to consider. I just want to get moving, taking wise steps to battle this cancer. Help me, Lord, to make wise decisions and trust that Your purpose will prevail.

You will complete the work that You began in me, and Your timing is perfect. You see the beginning from the end and everything in between. Thank You for building my faith so that I know I fight this battle with Your unfailing love and mercy.

Two more consults today. Help us to consider what is recommended and choose a plan that is good and honors You. You work through modern medicine and good nutrition. But ultimately it is You who does the healing.

July 20th, 2005

Yesterday, as I walked Westview Road—what a wonderful reminder of Your faithfulness. The miles and hours I logged on that road, the better part of eight years where You met me. I was so young and clueless, but You gently and faithfully guided me as You allowed me to dream, to wonder, to cry out to You in frustration, to long for "normal" times. Yes "we" have a history on Westview Road! The joy of remembering was so very sweet. Of course, the road is paved now and there are lots more homes, but in the 1970s, it was "our" special place where I heard You speak to me in my soul and You listened to me as I prayed for Mike, Molly, Maggie, for the Packer wives' Bible Study, and tons of other things. It was the place of beginnings, and now 34 years later, I reflected on Your grace and faithfulness—it was so very sweet. The place where I rocked my first baby. Like coming home to a place you began and sitting in the old chair where your daddy held you and told you stories and how much he loved you. It was awesome! And I thought You loved me then, but now I know!

July 22nd, 2012

From Pennsylvania, thankful for a safe journey yesterday. Long, but safe. Mike is sharing at First Baptist, and we'll get to visit with Esther and Randy for which I am very grateful.

One full day here before returning to Georgia tomorrow. Maggie has been such a help! Bless her with some rest in the midst of this busy visit. Keep Jeff safely in Your care.

July 24th, 2012

Back home. Brief but special visit in Pennsylvania and New York with the Elliotts and Brautigans. Smooth travel yesterday and first radiation treatment. I was so blessed to be given Mike's first class seat and no discomfort while traveling—amazing! The toughest part of the day was the 45 minutes of laying there with my left leg frog-legged while they took pictures, radiation pain down the outside of the leg. I kept praying for endurance and was so grateful for Your presence.

Now the routine kicks in for the next five weeks. Help me to take one day at a time and to enjoy the journey. This is the reality of countless people of all ages. Each case is unique. Thank You for reminding me that my faith is not in the treatment—it is in You! You are my Physician, my Refuge, and my Strength. In You alone do I trust.

Romans 8:38-39
For I am convinced that neither death nor life, neither angels nor demons, neither the present nor the future, nor any powers, neither height nor depth, nor anything else in all creation, will be able to separate us from the love of God that is in Christ Jesus our Lord.

I do ask Your tender mercy for Angie Bundy as she continues to struggle with headaches and lack of sleep! And for others who are facing discomfort, pain, and uncertainty. May they keep their confidence in You.

Off for a walk.

July 25th, 2012

Good morning, Lord. I love how You awaken my ears to listen. With all the ideas and life for me to process, it's so assuring to know that You are all wise and ever-present in my life.

Yesterday's treatment was better but still longer than planned as they had to reboot the computer! The drive was without delay, but it does take time. And remembering where the car is parked is critical to a stress-free exit.

It's good to be able to be home, even though it is a drive. Sleeping in my own bed and having my sweet morning time with You in this "happy place." Thank You for Your amazing goodness and favor.

And grant my dear friends Randy and Esther the ability to praise You even in their most difficult situations. Give them wisdom to know what to do and what to say and not say, for Your honor and glory.

Keep me fully committed to You in the midst of this season—that I may honor You by seeking Your help and receiving Your strength. Even as doctors and other professionals give their advice, I pray it is always filtered through the perspective of Your sovereignty.

So, off to the day You have made. Let me rejoice and be glad in it.

July 26th, 2012

Yesterday was so much better. The drive to midtown and treatment went so smoothly. My morning walk was pretty uncomfortable with my knee. It seems better today.

Lord, thank You for Jayde and how You have worked in her life and situation, and that she is such an encouragement. It was a blessing to talk to her and have her pray for Mike and me.

As Jason and Kylie prepare to return to the states, I pray that You show them signs of Your goodness in undeniable ways. May their trip go smoothly and quickly as they reflect on all that You did in and through them during this time.

Thank You for this day. You are worthy of all praise.

Lord, I submit to Your righteousness, Your sovereignty, Your wisdom, and I know that You richly bless all who call on You. Continue to give me discernment in my diet choices, that I make wise decisions that will be the best for me, not based on someone's opinions, and You know there are varying ones out there.

Surprise call from Rose yesterday. She said she hadn't heard my voice for ten days!

July 27th, 2012

It is Friday—day five of treatment. Awoke this morning craving oatmeal, my goodness gracious. Taking a day off from walking as the discomfort isn't worth it. I do ask for relief, should see the doctor on Tuesday.

Fun trip to the DeKalb Farmer's Market yesterday, seeing all the produce, fish, etc. And the whole world shopping or working there. Amazing, but pretty exhausting because it added to our trip.

Continued gratitude that I can trust You to care for me even
when my emotions surprise me. Keep faithful reminders to me
of Your Word, my very life, I ask.

2 Chronicles 20:15, 17
*"Do not be afraid or discouraged because of this vast army. For the
battle is not yours but God's. . . . Take up your positions; stand firm
and see the deliverance the* LORD *will give you . . . Do not be afraid;
do not be discouraged. Go out and face them tomorrow, and the*
LORD *will be with you."*

Your message is always: do not fear! Regardless of the enemy,
You ask that I stand firm and see the deliverance You provide.

July 27ᵗʰ, 2001

You tell me to, *"Stand at the crossroads and look;
ask for the ancient paths, ask where the good way is,
and walk in it, and you will find rest for your souls"*
(*Jeremiah 6:16*).

In following Your voice there is rest for my soul. My
goal is to be blameless—that Your Spirit would so
indwell me as to eliminate anything that is offensive
to You. Only in You will I find rest for my soul and
satisfaction.

July 28ᵗʰ, 2012

Another challenging treatment yesterday—the positions of my
leg—but the first week is over! Thank You, Lord, for sustaining

me through this and being my Shield. As I place my hand on my thigh and ask You to put a hedge of protection around this tumor and apply Your healing touch, I rest in the confidence that You will do what is best for me.

More decisions about the herbs with the doctors. I guess I'll suspend during treatment. Continue to give us discernment and wisdom I pray.

Expecting Jason and Kylie back on American soil this morning. Continue to wrap them all with Your comfort and protection.

This day, I choose to worship You in the midst of all the uncertainties and confusions. You alone are my God. You alone have sustained me and protected me with Your unequaled power and compassion.

You are my God in whom I trust. You are able to do exceedingly and abundantly more than I can ask or imagine. Nothing is too difficult for You!

July 29th, 2012

Yesterday, was rough. So much of the day I just sat on the couch. So good to have Katie and the kids here for a brief visit! I welcome them in Your name and pray that even in my limited capacity I can build into their memories a reflection of You!

Going to GCC today. I'm sure it will seem like a short drive compared to midtown. For all the pastors who are proclaiming Your Word today, I pray Your Spirit to help them proclaim clearly Your absolute truth.

July 30th, 2012

It's Monday. Enjoyed seeing dear friends yesterday and being
encouraged. Thank You for sweet sisters who pray—Jeannine
praying Psalm 91 and 27 for me:

Psalm 27:13-14
*I am still confident of this: I will see the goodness of the LORD in the land
of the living.*
Wait for the LORD; be strong and take heart and wait for the LORD.

I do love this reminder. I have seen so much of Your goodness in
the land of the living, amazing compassion and tenderness. Oh, to
dwell on Your faithfulness and goodness as I wait for You. Give me
the strength I need to wait.

July 31st, 2012

So thankful for sleep after a rough session yesterday. Going to try
narcotics prior to each radiation session. Talk about not expecting
this—we even have the professionals puzzled! But Lord, You knew,
and know and have me firmly gripped, 19 more sessions to go.

We still continue to be bombarded by differences of opinion,
and we need Your wisdom to sort through the options. Thank You
that You are the Giver of wisdom and direction and hope that does
not disappoint.

august 2012

August 1ˢᵗ, 2012

Thankful that Caleb made it to Cleveland and Carl was able to pick him up. Bless him for his service! That's amazing that he would do that. And Caleb is safely on U. S. soil. My heart is full of gratitude for the ways You show You care for us. Yesterday, I had four technicians assisting me at my treatment. And with the pill's effects I was able to endure. This is certainly not what I expected, but it is my reality. Knowing every case is different and each person is unique, still You are God and Author and Creator and Sustainer of all. You have my best interests in Your plans.

As the Brooks family prepares to say their final good-byes to India, and her Church family celebrates her life, I pray You give them strength and comfort, that everything said would honor You.

Thank You for this day and for the sweet memories of the last couple of days with Katie, Rody, and Ann Kate. Even though my limitations were so obvious, it was still fun to be with them and enjoy their very different personalities.

Lord, You are gracious and compassionate to all who turn to You. There are untold blessings from seeking You with all my heart. And now is a time—a season of unfamiliar paths—and I desperately need Your guidance and perspective, Your wisdom to make decisions in areas where I have opinions. You have blessed me with discernment, and I ask that You continue to keep me alert in this dimension. My only hope is in You!

Romans 15:4, 13
For everything that was written in the past was written to teach us, so that through endurance and the encouragement of the Scriptures we might have hope.
May the God of hope fill you with all joy and peace as you trust in him, so that you may overflow with hope by the power of the Holy Spirit.

Today Lord, I ask for Your gifts of endurance and encouragement. My hope is in You.

August 2nd, 2012

Traveling mercies, I pray, for the Evans' family today as they travel to Pennsylvania. Give them another bunch of sweet family camp memories this year, I ask. And for the Barnetts as they prepare to travel tomorrow. Hopefully, next year, we'll all be camping together again. I ask that You bless Mike with encouragement as he misses this annual time with family on the lake. We were just discussing this morning how our present reality doesn't seem real. But it is, and You are with us in it as we navigate and adjust. We're relying on You for our daily strength and endurance. You are faithful!

2 Chronicles 32
Hezekiah encouraged his military officers by saying, *"Be strong and courageous. Do not be afraid or discouraged because of the king of Assyria and the vast army with him, for there is greater power with us then with him. With him is only the arm of flesh, but with us is the LORD our God to help us and fight our battles."*

This helped the people gain confidence and yes, me too. No matter the enemy I face, in this case cancer, which is only flesh. You are God and the Lord who fights my battles, and You are able to conquer anything. No enemy stands a chance against You who gives life and controls death.

Interesting time with Dr. Jeff yesterday. Tapping on my head, seems a bit weird, but it's another approach to health. I trust You, Lord, to work through, or around, all these approaches that attempt to restore my health. My eyes are on You.

August 2nd, 2011

You gave Hezekiah opportunity to give You recognition when the rulers of Babylon came to ask him about the miraculous sign, and thus 15 more years of life proved the pride in his heart.

I'm just remembering that it was 15 years ago when my parents moved to Georgia, and in February, it will be 15 years since my cancer surgery.

All the blessings I've experienced these 15 years are all from Your hand, and even in the difficulties, You have always been faithful. Let me be aware of opportunities to give You praise for all this and not to let my heart become proud. May I take every opportunity to bring encouragement to those I encounter. Help me to recognize seeds of pride and repent at every occasion.

August 3rd, 2012

Day 10 of treatment, going this morning due to schedule changes. I'm really ready for a couple of days off. Thinking of Reese at the Olympics today and praying Your favor on his efforts. It's been fun to watch the competition during this past week, a special treat.

Bless Karin Thomas for her sweet note received yesterday. I have been strengthened and encouraged by so many who are praying for me. Thank You for listening to their pleas, and mine. I praise You with my utmost being remembering all Your benefits—You forgive my sins and heal my disease. You redeem my life from the pit and crown me with love and compassion. You satisfy my desires with good things so my youth is renewed. You are my ever-loving, faithful God.

August 4th, 2012

So it's move-in day at Camp Fitch today. Hate that I'm not there to be a part of it, but I pray for each family member who is, that You would give them lots of sweet family memories to bless them with the awareness of Your goodness. This truly is a gift from You.

Feeling a little discouraged today as I couldn't get comfortable in bed last night so I slept on the couch. But I did sleep! And I'm giving in to the narcotics to see if that will give me the relief I need, because the ibuprofen sure isn't helping with the swelling.

And I pray for Angie Bundy as she continues to battle headaches and other issues. Give her relief I pray.

My plea is for wisdom for the doctors, as all this was so not on my radar and certainly not what was even hinted at to expect. Have mercy, I ask. I need strength and encouragement, and I look forward to being with You in Your Word now, for Your Word is my very life.

August 2ⁿᵈ, 2004

As I look back, as far as I can, in my family I see Rose Secoy Moore and her faith, a life that lasted 31 years, her daughter, Gladys, who was left at nine years old with no more training in godliness then at 77 getting "reacquainted with an old friend." Thank You, Father, for the glimpse, what a treasure! She entered eternity with the truth of Your Word. Thank You for restarting faith in me and my family. Help me to encourage my children to follow You wholeheartedly.

August 5ᵗʰ, 2012

Yesterday, was pretty rough. Stayed on regimen of narcotics and ibuprofen while on the couch all day and night. Today I feel okay, just a little battle weary. I couldn't even do any reading yesterday.

The kids are settled in at Camp Fitch, and I know they're having a good time. Keep them safe and happy, I pray!

Thank You for Your new mercies today. Every good and perfect gift comes from You.

As Your Word is proclaimed in the house of worship today, I pray for hearts to be open and lives to be transformed. And for those who are Yours who are wandering, I pray Your mercy and conviction to lead them back to the safety of Your Lordship.

August 6th, 2012

Another week begins. Yesterday, was more comfortable than Saturday. So many praying for me and I know You're listening. Even when I can't pray for myself, You are reminded of my needs through their pleas.

Talked with Mother. Always hard as she tries so hard but just doesn't connect with me. Good to talk with Diane and Jayde. I know Jayde knows my journey even though each is different. Guide her as she prepares a talk about her journey to be shared on August 14th.

I do ask You to give the doctor wisdom today as she sees me for the first time since radiation began. Fresh from her vacation, rested eyes and mind to make the best evaluation for me. It's hard to believe that three months ago I was preparing for Oberstdorf and concerned about my saw/loop combo. Now here I am before Your throne asking for mercy in the scary battle with cancer. You are my ever-present God in whom I place all my trust!

August 7th, 2012

More changes to my regimen. Adding morphine every twelve hours to see if having something in my system as a time release will manage the pain better. Treatment was a bit rough as the machine had to be rebooted. The technicians were very nice though and I survived.

It's good that the doctor is back—good to talk through details with her. And so good to have steak fajita last night, a special treat!

I keep reminding myself that my hope is built on nothing less than Jesus' blood and righteousness. And I beg for endurance and encouragement.

Facing the reality that I won't be going to California or Ireland as planned. A man makes his plans, but the Lord directs his steps—You have complete authority to do so. In so many ways You have blessed me, in surprising ways that have made me just laugh with delight. Knowing I can trust You to do what is best for me is the most secure place I know.

Thank You, Lord, for Your tender and sufficient and new mercies today. I ask that You keep my family safe at Fitch and give them lots to smile about!

Psalm 29:11
The LORD gives strength to his people; the LORD blesses his people with peace.

August 8th, 2012

Another day, another dilemma for the medical community. Trying to resolve my swelling issue. Give them wisdom beyond ability, I ask, as they seek to resolve. And as always, I am grateful for sleep!

Thankful to hear from Molly that all is going well at Fitch. The Olympic competition sounds like fun. Continue to bless them with special family times.

Early day today as I go for an MRI first and treatment at 1:30. Knowing You have me firmly gripped gives me hope!

August 9th, 2001

We are preparing to travel to Camp Fitch—for now our 17th time. It is our family's "Feast of Tabernacles" or "Ingathering." *Be joyful at your feast. . . For seven days celebrate the Feast to the LORD your God at the place the LORD will choose. For the LORD your God will bless you in all your harvest and in all the work of your hands, and your joy will be complete (Deuteronomy 16:14-15). Celebrate the festival to the LORD for seven days; the first is a day of rest, and the eighth day also is a day of rest. . . . Celebrate this as a festival to the LORD for seven days each year. This is to be a lasting ordinance for the generations to come (Leviticus 23:39, 41).*

As I wonder why all of us look forward to this time each year, I realize this too is a gift from You! May we celebrate Your faithfulness together in a way that honors You. I thank You for this time and this place that You have chosen!

August 20th, 2001

I thank You for the fun and safe celebration of the "Feast of Ingathering," as our family now refers to our annual time at Camp Fitch. For seven days, we live in tents at the place that that the Lord has chosen and celebrate His faithfulness! For 17 years, we have been blessed with this special time with family. This year my energies and efforts were mostly channeled toward Kylie and Kaitlyn. But I did get to bike ride to Tasty Twist with Katie and Maggie, have a brief morning visit with Esther, listen to Aunt Jean's stories, and take a night hike with Katie, Maggie, Molly, and Jason. The special joy of seeing Larry, Kaitlyn's counselor, come to faith in Christ. He was baptized in "calm" Lake Erie on August 16th.

Thank You, Father, that I can trust You, that You have given me Your Word that is living and active, sharper than a two-edged sword, that is profitable for reproof, training in righteousness, and correction. Your Word teaches me, empowers me, and sustains me. Let me not forsake You. Teach me Your way and give me an undivided heart, that the words of my mouth and the meditations of my heart would be pleasing to You!

August 9th, 2012

Oh my, what a day yesterday. MRI was much more than I anticipated, between drugs and Your encouragement, I made it through the over one-hour process. I know it was especially difficult for Mike as he imagined how much pain I was in. It's so hard when you can't do anything and want desperately to do so.

News from the MRI wasn't good. Tumor is growing, swelling not from radiation effects—there's some kind of bleed going on. Waiting for Dr. O. to look at the films and give his opinion. I've been praying for wisdom as medical minds collaborate. You know what's best for me; give Your guidance to those who have a stake in this treatment.

August 11th, 2012

Even more overwhelmed today as now chemo is recommended to try to shrink this tumor. So Monday I will go to the hospital for 4.5 days to begin a one-drug chemo and complete radiation in the next two weeks.

This is so much more than we ever expected! Your mercy, I pray, for all of us. And Your grace to endure whatever is ahead.

Update #1
Prayer Request
August 14th, 2012

I just wanted to send out a quick prayer request for my mom. Last week my mom finished her third week of radiation. She experienced some unusual swelling and pain, to the point where she can't walk anymore. She had an MRI last week, and it showed that the tumor in her leg had grown considerably in the last month and closer to her femur bone. They think the growth is pinching nerves and that's what is causing the pain. Since the tumor is not responding to the radiation treatment, she was admitted to the hospital this morning.

She'll start chemotherapy treatments tomorrow for five days—it will be added to the radiation—and will come home on Saturday. Next week she'll finish her last week of radiation. And then, the week following, she'll go back to the hospital for a week of chemotherapy and will be back home for three weeks. This process will continue for the next four-and-a-half months. After the four-and-a-half months, they'll have surgery to make a clean removal of the tumor.

Please pray that the side effects will not be severe and that she'll have an appetite to enjoy my wonderful cooking.

Thank you!
Caleb

August 29th, 2012

Dear sweet Karson is ten today. I remember so well the day he was born and have so many cherished memories of time with him. Thank You, Lord.

So it's time for another journal, as my hair begins to fall out and I'm on this journey of a real battle. I'm learning that the dictates of cancer can change everything and that the schedule is always subject to change!

At least I'm beginning to be able to think somewhat clearly at times and to realize that nothing can or will separate me from Your love, even the fog of drugs. How I praise You for Your faithfulness!

2 Timothy 3:16-17
All scripture is God-breathed and is useful for teaching, rebuking, correcting and training in righteousness so that the man of God may be thoroughly equipped for every good work.

Psalm 94:19
When anxiety was great within me, your consolation brought joy to my soul.

Your Word and the reminders of what You have taught me through years of just spending time in it with You continues to bring comfort to my soul in the midst of this season. I cannot explain the peace, the perspective, that You continue to surround me with. I'm taking each day as a gift, enjoying each breath, and being aware that You are my great reward and my ever-present God.

Not a minute in Your Word has ever been without effect. Your Word will stand, as Jeremiah says. Of this I am confident; You who began a good work in me will complete it, like Paul reminds us in Philippians 1:6. Thank You for that assurance.

september 2012

Update #2
September 6th, 2012

Hello everyone,

I just wanted to update you guys on the latest with my mom. She finished her first chemo treatment two-and-a-half weeks ago that was going to help the last two weeks of her radiation. She spent the last two weeks at home resting. She needed a blood transfusion and a couple trips to the ER battling a high fever. Her appetite remained good. She enjoyed my cooking as well as a few meals from friends. After many experiments, I think I will enter my strawberry banana Jell-O into the next World Jell-O Competition.

This past Friday, my mom had an MRI done on her leg and a scan of her lungs. Yesterday, we found out the results of those tests. Her sarcoma had grown a centimeter since her last MRI on August 8th. It is now 15 centimeters. There is now a second satellite tumor—it's five centimeters and is very aggressive. They found five spots on her lungs earlier in the summer that haven't grown, but there is a new spot that has shown up. They don't know at this point whether the spots are cancer.

This morning, we met with the oncology surgeon and he suggested surgery. So, tomorrow afternoon my mom will have surgery to remove her sarcomas. He will try and save her leg by taking out the sarcomas and rebuilding her femur with titanium rods. If he feels that he can't get good margins, then he will do an amputation.

If he has a chance at saving the leg, the doctors will do a pathology report on the sarcoma. It usually takes a week to ten days to get the results. If the pathologist thinks that the margins were not good, then she'll have another surgery two weeks from tomorrow to amputate the leg. If the doctors are able to save her leg and the margins are good, then Mom will be able to start chemo in two weeks. The chemo will be done for four months to kill any cancer that could've metastasized. If Mom has the amputation, she'll have to wait six weeks for the wound to heal before starting chemo.

Please pray for tomorrow's surgery and for God's guidance and wisdom for the doctor.

Please pray that the spots on my mom's lungs are not cancer.

Whatever befalls,
Caleb

Update #3
September 8ᵗʰ, 2012

Dear family and friends,

First of all, thank you so much for your prayers! I had some time this morning to read your emails with words of encouragement, written prayers, verses.

My mom went through four hours of surgery yesterday. The doctor feels like he got clean margins. He had to take all of her quadriceps muscle and replace her entire femur with a titanium rod. We will know the pathology report of the sarcoma in five days. Please be praying those results will be positive so she will not have to go back for surgery.

I just got back from the hospital and she is still drugged but able to eat. As for when she'll be able to come home, it all depends on her pain control. Hopefully by Monday or Tuesday.

Please keep praying. It is still going to be a battle, but we finally feel we are starting to take the hill.

I will send out another update next week when we
know the results of the pathology.

Be blessed,
Caleb

Update #4
September 14ᵗʰ, 2012

Hello all,

Today is a good day! After watching the Green Bay
Packer highlights from last night, a great fake field goal
for a touchdown, and snacking on some gluten-free
chocolate chip cookies, the nurse came in and told us
the doctor just called. The pathology report came back
with negative margins, meaning that all the tissue taken
from around the sarcoma had no cancer cells! Thank
You, Jesus! The doctor should be doing rounds this
afternoon and we should know the type of sarcoma.

We are hoping to go home sometime this weekend. We
are still working on Mom's pain management. They had
to lengthen her leg a bit in order to give her hip a little
more stability when she starts walking, because she will
be using her hip and backside muscles to walk. When
they lengthened her leg with the titanium rod, they had
to stretch out her sciatic nerve. That is what has been
causing her the most pain. The pain management doctor
came in this morning and will be changing around her
meds. Once those are stable and she can move around
a bit more without pain, she will be able to come home.

We will most likely be doing in-home health for her physical therapy. Once she starts moving around easier, we will look at the next step for treatment.

If anyone would like to make a visit, please contact me and I will organize that.

Please keep praying.
Caleb

Update #5
Welcome Home, Ma!
September 19th, 2012

Good morning!

Mom was honorably discharged from the hospital yesterday. We left just in time to avoid any traffic, and after twelve days in the hospital, it was nice to be home. Our friend Peggy came over and helped us settle back in. She also brought over a "Welcome Home Kia" cake from Dairy Queen. We must never forget to celebrate the small accomplishments with cake!

Our friend Peyton brought over some homemade chili and cornbread, and after celebrating with cake (I celebrated several times), we fell asleep watching the Braves' game.

Last night was the first time in two months my mom was able to sleep in her bed. She is still working on walking more and more with her walker. She will start in-home physical therapy in the next several days. But today, it will be PT McCoy putting her through the workout. I think after some eggs benedict à la Caleb, she will be ready to go.

I just wanted to thank everyone once again for your prayers!

She has an appointment to see the surgeon this Monday morning to get her staples out and check everything over. We will also be discussing the next steps in treatment.

Please continue to pray for healing. Please continue to pray that the spots in her lungs will disappear and all other cancer cells hiding in her body will disappear.

Please pray for wisdom and strength as we continue down this road.

Y'all have a wonderful day!
Caleb

September 20th, 2004

Until I asked You to give me a hunger and thirst for Your Word, I only had a vague idea of You. I have now seen Your consistent character throughout Your dealings with us and that all You have promised will be fulfilled. I have heard You say "I love you" so many times in so many ways and "thanks for visiting, stop by anytime you're in the neighborhood" just like my daddy used to say.

You've even given me a glimpse into the faith of my great-grandmother, Rose Secoy Moore. I look forward to meeting her someday. Her 31 years seemed so short, but Your purpose for her was fulfilled. You allowed me to re-introduce her daughter, my grandmother, to an old friend, Jesus, some 70 years after her death. Who but You could have planned that? Thank You for the honor of the ministry and purpose for which You have called me!

September 24ᵗʰ, 2007

Again my cup overflows with amazement and blessings! The time at the retreat was so good and You obviously spoke to me, through me, and the ladies. Being able to share my heritage of faith, recently discovered, and the legacy of faith being established. Time with Esther and Randy and with the Bethel folks was such a blessing.

Arriving at the airport expecting openings on the early flight that I was led to believe on Thursday, and being met with a full plane where I was allowed to stand by but without the twenty-five dollar charge. Tempted to count each traveler as they entered the gate area, I continued to pray Your favor, and You abundantly provided not only space on the Philadelphia flight, but a much earlier Atlanta flight, confirmed, at no additional cost. As I sit in 10D, praising You for Your goodness and faithfulness, I look at the head of the young man directly in front of me wearing a Levi-Straus cap with 1873 on the back staring me at eye level. Wow! Rose Secoy Moore born in 1873, the year in her Bible, as far back as I can trace my faith heritage! I almost burst into tears. It may seem like a very small thing, but I know You orchestrated it too in one more way to remind me of Your faithfulness.

Thank You, Lord. I love You and I love how You love me.

Isaiah 45:3
I will give you the hidden treasures, riches stored in secret places, so that you may know that I am the Lord, the God of Israel, who summons you by name.

Update #6
September 27th, 2012

Good evening family, (Yes, we're all family!)

Mom had her post-operation checkup this afternoon. Her 58 staples were taken out—so she's one step closer to soaking in the bubble bath.

Right now, Mom will concentrate each day on getting her leg stronger and becoming more and more independent. She has already made leaps and bounds in the past eight days since coming home from the hospital. She is eating all her meals at the dining table while sitting in her wheelchair. She does her daily tour around the kitchen and dining room with her walker. For tomorrow's morning therapy walk, I will try and get her into the garage to sort through all the things stored above the garage that I brought down. We are having a neighborhood garage sale this Saturday. So, if you would like to come buy our stuff, stop on by ole Cotton Gin Row. If you spend more than $20, you get a free shaker weight! Can't beat that!

We have about four more weeks to consider our chemotherapy options. The doctor thinks she will be strong enough to start treatment by that time. I like to look at it as that we all have four more weeks to pray for healing.

Never cease,
Caleb

october 2012

Update #7
October 5th, 2012

This past Monday we went to see a new oncologist for a second opinion. On October 15th, Mom will have a scan of her lungs. On October 16th we'll know if the spot that showed up on the August 31st scan has grown. If it has grown, then we'll know it is the sarcoma. Even though my mom had her sarcoma removed from her leg, there is a very good chance that it will show up again because it was a stage three aggressive sarcoma. Chemotherapywillnotcuremymom'ssarcoma.Whether or not my mom goes through four months of chemo, the sarcoma will come back at some point. The chemo will only have a 30-percent chance of slowing any growth of the sarcoma in the lung—if it happens to be that. And it will only have a 30-percent chance of killing any microscopic sarcoma cells hiding out somewhere that haven't shown up yet. Hard facts.

For the first time two days ago, Mom walked from the kitchen to her bedroom. She no longer needs help pushing her foot forward. As of today, I made the wheelchair off-limits in the bedroom—she'll have to walk into her bedroom from here on out. Hopefully by next week, she will be wheelchair free!

Please keep praying.
Caleb

Update #8
October 17ᵗʰ, 2012

Hello all,

I really don't know how to start this.

We went to see the oncologist this morning in Athens. The sarcoma has spread to Mom's lungs. The spots that showed up on her last scan have now doubled in size in the past six weeks, as well as with some new ones showing up. My mom will be getting another scan in four weeks to see if the sarcoma continues at the same growth rate.

The chemotherapy treatment for sarcoma has a 30-percent chance that it will slow the growth. This 30-percent is a number that doctors have put out there because there haven't been enough studies done on sarcoma. None have been done on "stage three" sarcomas—the stage my mom is in. The doctor is concerned about doing more chemotherapy because of the reaction Mom had to a low-dose single drug at the end of her radiation. We asked what Mom's life expectancy would be if she decided not to do chemo. He said six months would be a generous estimation at the current growth rate of the sarcoma. Even if we tried the chemo, there is no guarantee of prolonging life. Before the doctor left the room, my dad asked if he could pray.

During my dad's prayer he said he was thankful for Mom's healing—the healing she experienced when she accepted the Lord Jesus into her heart.

I have never looked at it that way before. This whole time we have been praying for healing while the whole time she has already been healed. The forgiveness of our sins is the greatest miracle.

One day there will be no more sickness, no more pain. We will be made perfect.

Whatever befalls,
Caleb

October 25th, 2012

Happy Birthday dear Kasen—two years old. Memories of your arrival flood my heart with joy—you were such a welcome surprise! And how you've daily brought joy to our world by your sweet presence. Oh, how I cherish the memories of being with you in March of this year while your family went to D. C. We had two-and-a-half days together alone and you delighted my soul by your actions and interactions. You truly are a *joy*!

Thank You, Lord, for bringing this dear child into our family. May he continue to grow in grace as he gets older and bring him to a knowledge of You!

October 29th, 2001

Jesus, Your words, let me hear them, let me see with eyes of enlightenment, let my heart understand what You are saying to me and showing me through my daily bread of Your Word. I come today without money and I purchase. Redeem my time with the abundance of nourishment for the needs of my soul. Your eyes are open to all my ways!

november 2012

November 1st, 2012

Delightful reminder.

Lamentations 3:22-26
Because of the LORD's great love we are not consumed, for his compassions never fail. They are new every morning; great is your faithfulness. I say to myself, "The LORD is my portion; therefore I will wait for him." The LORD is good to those whose hope is in him, to the one who seeks him; it is good to wait quietly for the salvation of the LORD.

Lord, thank You for Your new mercies this morning. You indeed are my portion, and I rest in Your goodness as I reflect in awe of it.

November 4th, 2012

Lord, I am so grateful for Anne—she is such a blessing. I pray You
bless and encourage her as she has been such a blessing to me, being
here several days, cooking and serving me, and just being a special
light of Your love. Even though I lost a pound this week, I did eat
well and had such tasty meals and snacks.

Hebrews 4:16
*Let us then [because of Jesus] approach the throne of grace with
confidence, so that we may receive mercy and find grace to help us in our
time of need.*

Jesus, You are my great High Priest who has gone through the
heavens and are able to sympathize with my weaknesses.

Because of Jesus' reverent submission to You, His prayers, cries and
tears, were heard. He learned obedience from what he suffered and
became the source of eternal salvation.

James 1:2
Consider it pure joy, my brothers, whenever you face trials of many kinds.

Psalm 100:4
*Enter his gates with thanksgiving and his courts with praise; give thanks
to him and praise his name.*

I can bless God—not take anything, ask anything, demand
anything.

And when Jesus knew He was going to die and celebrated the last
supper with His disciples, He served them, blessed them, and
encouraged them.

Mom at the age of 12 in Troy, New York

Mom's senior picture in 1967

The Spaldings, L-R, Monica, Kevin, Dave, Kia, Brian, Rose

Showing off her fancy costume in
1967 with Ice Capades

Dad's rookie year in Green Bay, 1970

Mom, Grandpa Dave, Grandma Rose, and Monica

Mom's last walk on the shores of Lake Erie with Maggie in July 2012

Dave's girls

Grandma Kia holding David McCoy Barnett
shortly after birth on December 21st, 2012. Coy is
her seventh grandbaby.

The whole clan. First row L-R. Kasen, Kaitlyn, Grandma Kia, Grandpa, Anna Kate, Rody.
Second row L-R. Jason, Molly, Caleb, Karson, Kylie, Maggie, Jeff, Katie (pregnant with
baby Coy), Randy. Christy Martin Photography

The kids, L-R, Caleb, Katie, Maggie, Molly. Christy Martin Photography

The Grandkids, L-R, Rody, Karson, Kaitlyn, Kylie, Kasen, Anna
Kate. Christy Martin Photography

43 years of marriage
Christy Martin
Photography

Kaitlyn and Grandma Kia showing off
their hats in November 2012. Christy
Martin Photography

Mom walking Westview Road in Suamico, Wisconsin in July 2005

July 20th, 2005

Yesterday as I walked Westview Road—what a wonderful reminder of Your faithfulness. The miles and hours I logged on that road, the better part of eight years where You met me. I was so young and clueless, but You gently and faithfully guided me as You allowed me to dream, to wonder, to cry out to You in frustration, to long for "normal" times. Yes "we" have a history on Westview Road! The joy of remembering was so very sweet. Of course the road is paved now and there are lots more homes, but in the 1970s, it was "our" special place where I heard You speak to me in my soul and You listened to me as I prayed for Mike, Molly, Maggie, for the Packer wives' Bible Study, and tons of other things. It was the place of beginnings and now 34 years later, I reflected on Your grace and faithfulness and it was so very sweet. The place where I rocked my first baby. Like coming home to a place you began and sitting in the old chair where your daddy held you and told you stories and how much he loved you. It was awesome! And I thought You loved me then, but now I know!

Kia's bench overlooking Lake Erie at Camp Fitch

September 1st, 2008
Isaiah 60:19-22
The sun will no more be your light by day, nor will the brightness of the moon shine on you,
for the Lord will be your everlasting light, and your God will be your glory.
Your sun will never set again, and your moon will wane no more;
the Lord will be your everlasting light, and your days of sorrow will end. . . .
I am the Lord; in its time I will do this swiftly.

I think of the sunsets we've watched in amazement—each different in its own way. And now to be reminded that this will only last for a time before You become my everlasting light and glory.

The time is coming when sunrises, sunsets, moonlit skies will be a thing of the past—not even a memory—in comparison to You. I can't even imagine! In its time, You will do this swiftly, when the nets are full.

How the news that I have a malignancy in my leg is not what I expected to hear! And so this journey begins of consults, tests, plans — but as I drove to SC yesterday in the quiet, all I could think was to praise you — that I knew that I know You are sovereign over

my life & death & welfare — and that whatever the future holds, I know you've got me firmly in your grip! I am at peace —

I ask that you help us to just rest in your care, give the doctors wisdom beyond their ability —

So many plans have been made and now it's all on hold as we wait to hear the details —

As I walked to the mailbox this morning & breathed in the fresh air — I am aware of how healthy I feel apart from my quad. So, I am thankful for that blessing! —

Her beautiful handwriting from July 7th, 2012

He served those who He loved. Help me, Lord, to bless others in the time I have left—that I can be an encouragement, that what I have learned of You I can pass on to others. I ask for ideas and words that will be impactful and for lasting memories.

Hebrews 6:17-20
Because God wanted to make the unchanging nature of his purpose very clear to the heirs of what was promised, he confirmed it with an oath. God did this so that, by two unchangeable things, in which it is impossible for God to lie, we who have fled to take hold of the hope offered to us may be greatly encouraged. We have this hope as an anchor for the soul, firm and secure. It enters the inner sanctuary behind the curtain, where Jesus, who went before us has entered on our behalf. He has become a high priest forever.

My soul is anchored in the hope You provide, Lord, firm and secure. It was such a blessing to talk with Martha Spalding yesterday. I pray You protect her as she travels back to Wisconsin and that You give her clear direction in the days ahead. I know she is disappointed that her hand issue won't allow her to continue her course work in Dallas, but You can and will use her to serve You elsewhere. Thank You for the healing You have provided during her seminary days and for the firm foundation in Your Word that she has received during her studies.

Some thoughts from *One Thousand Gifts* by Ann Voskamp:

- The only place we need to see before we die is the place of seeing God, here and now. Joy is possible, as long as there is thanksgiving!
- What is the significance of God touching Jacob upon the sinew of his thigh? The sinew of the thigh is the strongest in the human body; a horse could not even tear it apart.

So, the Lord has to break us down at the strongest part of
ourselves, before He can have His own way of blessing us.

- Wrestling with God, pleading for understanding to see. The
secret to joy is to keep seeking God where we doubt He is.
There's no seeing God face-to-face without first the ripping.
Seeing Him is the ultimate blessing. It's joy in the desert.

- The feeling of joy begins with the action of thanksgiving;
joy comes from the place of the very presence of God.

- The demanding of my own will is the singular force that
smoothes out joy.

- The full moon. I have always been awed by it and hopefully
have transferred that to my children and grandchildren. I
remember the full moon rising over the Atlantic at Hilton
Head one June, absolutely breathtaking. I've grown to
appreciate the wonder of God's creation so much that I put
the dates of the yearly full moons on my calendar; this year
one is on my birthday and also Molly's and Jason's.

The author tells of her thoughts around the full moon:

"Joy that fills me under a full moon is the joy that always fills God. . . .
God sees it all. This is His endless experience because this is who He
is, beauty overflowing. My moon wonder is but a glimpse, foretaste,
of what God always sees, experiences. . . . Joy is God's life." (p.117)

Joy fills me under a full moon too, reminding me of God's
faithfulness and the wonder of His dependability, an obvious sign
of His trustworthiness.

June 21st, 2000

It's the first day of summer, and we are enjoying a
beautiful week at Hilton Head. My day began with

a beach bike ride with Kylie. Thank You for the two beautiful full moon nights at the beach. It was as if You did all that just for me!

1 Chronicles 16:31-32
Let the heavens rejoice, let the earth be glad; let them say among the nations, "The LORD reigns!" Let the sea resound, and all that is in it.

September 16th, 2000

Just this week I see displayed another full moon and today I read.

Psalm 89:35-37
"Once for all, I have sworn by my holiness—and I will not lie to David—that his line will continue forever and his throne endure before me like the sun; it will be established forever like the moon, the faithful witness in the sky."

The moon is Your faithful witness in the sky of Your trustworthiness, Your holiness, Your dependability! Thank You for this awesome way to praise You!

November 1st, 2001

I've been amazed by the beauty of a full moon on a clear night and I realize that as I sit here it is night on the other side of the earth—Your works are displayed in every place. I pray that many would seek You as they see with their eyes the declaration of Your glory! I wonder

if David was looking at a full moon when he penned
the words to Psalm 19.

November 19th, 2002

As Caleb and I viewed the New England sky at eleven
last night watching for the anticipated Orion show—in
the beautiful clear, cold night with almost full moon—I
remembered David's words in Psalm 19:1-3:

*The heavens declare the glory of God; the skies proclaim the
work of his hands. Day after day they pour forth speech;
night after night they display knowledge. There is no speech
or language where their voice is not heard. Their voice goes
out into all the earth, their words to the ends of the world.*

A late night, bright lights that display Your glory right
before our eyes. Thank You for reminding me of Your
hand's work, not just a celestial phenomenon!

October 23rd, 2010

How I love how man tries to predict with such
confidence when only You know the days ordained for
us! I just ask Your favor and protection over Molly and
this new life and trust Your timing which is perfect.

How I rejoiced over the full moon last night as it rose
over the back of our house. Its brilliance shouted to me,
"Your God is faithful!" It is Your witness in the night
sky and it proclaims Your glory, the work of Your hands,
and I didn't miss the opportunity to praise You.

November 21ˢᵗ, 2010

This is the day You have made, I will rejoice and be glad in it. Thank You for the spectacular majesty displayed in the full moon last night that spoke to me of Your faithfulness and glory.

There is much on the schedule today. May You be honored in it all. Bless those who are traveling, and show Your compassion in obvious ways to those who are hurting. I just think of those who have lost loved ones or are facing their final holiday with family. Your yoke is easy and Your burden is light!

November 7ᵗʰ, 2012

This one thing I know: no matter how difficult it is to comprehend the events of this world, You are still and always will be on the throne!

Hebrews 7:24-27
Because Jesus lives forever, he has a permanent priesthood. Therefore he is able to save completely those who come to God through him, because he always lives to intercede for them. Such a high priest meets our need—one who is holy, blameless, pure, set apart from sinners, exalted above the heavens. . . . He sacrificed for their sins once for all when he offered himself.

Reminds me of studying Your Word with Susan Paynter, who has been with You now twelve years. The great assurance I have that You, Jesus, are interceding for me, my every need is being monitored before the very throne of God. I rest in Your promises.

November 8ᵗʰ, 2012

Monica and Dan are in Jordan. I pray for their protection and that they would be a blessing to the people at that hospital. Thank You for those who have invested their lives to help the helpless. Mike is in Kansas City at a Christo Ray school. I pray for open hearts and minds for the students to receive the hope that is offered.

Thank You for the unexpected and generous blessing from Mike's Thursday morning group that arrived yesterday, and for all the cards of encouragement I continue to receive. Today is another day I awake feeling good and strong! It is a good day indeed because You have ordained it and it is Yours. I will rejoice and be glad in it.

"For the Christian the beginning of the day should not be burdened and oppressed with besetting concerns for the day's work. At the threshold of each new day stands the Lord who made it, all the darkness and distraction of the dreams of night retreat before the clear light of Jesus Christ and His wakening Word. All unrest, all impurity, all care and anxiety flee before Him. Therefore, at the beginning of the day, let all distraction and empty talk be silenced and let the first thought and the first word belong to Him to whom our whole life belongs." Dietrich Bonhoeffer, *Life Together (p. 43)*

This is such a timely reminder of what my perspective should be. Regardless of circumstances, God is on the throne and nothing happens apart from His sovereign will—even the really hard stuff. Certainly Bonhoeffer faced some difficult challenges, and I'm grateful for his example and perspective!

Lord, let my first and last thought of every day belong to You, to whom my whole life belongs.

November 9th, 2012

Hebrews 9:24
For Christ did not enter a man-made sanctuary that was only a copy of the true one; he entered heaven itself, now to appear for us in God's presence.

Affirming Your presence, Jesus in heaven, for my benefit before God's throne is such an encouragement.

Psalm 107:28-29
Then they cried out to the LORD in their trouble, and he brought them out of their distress. He stilled the storm to a whisper; the waves of the sea were hushed.

I have loved the picture of You stilling a storm to a whisper. Raging winds and rain and thunder and lightning in the circumstances of my life become but a whisper in Your unfailing love.

November 13th, 2012

As Bonheoffer said, "the beginning of the day should not be burdened with the besetting concerns of the day." *Life Together* (p. 43) My whole life belongs to You, Lord, and all anxiety flees before You and Your Word. I have no fear of bad news for You are God!

I am ever grateful for the promises You guarantee in Your Word, for the consolation these bring to my soul. I have confidence to enter the most holy place by the blood of Jesus. I draw near to You with a sincere heart in full assurance of faith. Help me to hold unswervingly to this hope, for You who promised are faithful.

I know I have better and lasting possessions awaiting me. My confidence will be richly rewarded. Lord, I believe. Keep me strong, I pray.

Hebrews 11:6
Without faith it is impossible to please God, because anyone who comes to him must believe that he exists and that he rewards those who earnestly seek him.

Update #9
November 14th, 2012

Hello All,

Yesterday afternoon, I took Mom to Mayfield, and we celebrated life with a little bit of ice cream. My mom got some butter pecan, and I got some birthday cake. She has been on a pretty strict diet over the past month of no sugar, no wheat, and eating a lot of green veggies.

The results from yesterday's scan were that she still has no spots in her abdomen and pelvis. She has no new spots in her lungs, but the spots that she does have in her lungs are still growing at the same growth rate.

She is feeling great and looking great. She is getting around so much better. She can get in and out of bed all by herself. Yesterday, I was putting stuff in the car and turned around and she had already gotten herself in the backseat. Also, we spent most of the day in doctor's appointments, in and out of the car, and she never used the wheelchair. She walked everywhere with her walker. A first!

During the in-home therapy sessions, she is walking with two canes and started going up some stairs. She is getting pretty close to going to a physical therapy center. Mom decided not to do chemotherapy, and we have been doing some alternative treatments over the past month. Yesterday, we decided to do a gene testing that the doctor recommended. A tissue sample of her sarcoma that was taken from her leg will be sent to Boston, and they'll do tests on it. They'll determine what DNA strands have been affected, and this will determine if there are any clinical trials going on now that she would be a match for. There are several clinical trials going on for sarcoma, but she has to be a match for them. We would only choose ones that are close and involve no chemotherapy treatment. There is a potential that she wouldn't match any of the trials, but since there is so very little research on sarcoma, it would still be very beneficial to get tested for future research. Hopefully, one day, we can say my mom had a small part in being able to find a cure for sarcoma.

We also had an interesting afternoon yesterday. We saw a holistic herbalist medical doctor. He was born into the underground church in China. His grandfather was a preacher. In his town there was an American missionary who had an influential impact on their church. His last name was McCoy.

Next week, we are all looking forward to being together for Thanksgiving. Mom is already planning the gingerbread-house-making party for the six grandkids. We'll be having a family photo done next Saturday. It has been four years since our last one.

My sisters are planning some color coordination with each family. I will be wearing purple—the lone wolf.

In two weeks, we'll find out the results of the gene testing and see if she is a match for any of the trials. Please be praying for that and for the time we'll have as a family next week.

Still, my soul will sing . . .
Caleb

November 15ᵗʰ, 2012

I continue to feel good. It was interesting meeting with Dr. Cool and his wife Shirley the other day. Lying on my stomach for an hour was interesting and so was hearing his story of faith, beginning with a grandfather who was a bishop in the Chinese underground church. The soft music as I was hooked up to electrodes—seemingly—delighted my soul. "How Great Thou Art" was one of the songs, a favorite.

Psalm 112:7
He will have no fear of bad news; his hearts is steadfast, trusting in the LORD.

November 15ᵗʰ, 2001

You have entrusted this time to me: let me not criticize what happened in the past in my family, but take the challenge and responsibility to affect positively those who follow after me. That my life would be lived consistently with the truth of Your Word. You were there when my ancient ruins first crumbled—You know every detail, and You are a God that reconstructs. Oh, to be that link that takes my family line from the unfulfilling life of religion to a passionate life of relationship with Christ!

November 17th, 2012

I am loving Hebrews and the delightful reminders from Your Word.

Hebrews 12:28-29
Therefore, since we are receiving a kingdom that cannot be shaken, let us be thankful, and so worship God acceptably with reverence and awe, for our "God is a consuming fire."

Hebrews 13:15
Through Jesus, therefore, let us continually offer to God a sacrifice of praise—the fruit of lips that confess his name.

James 1:12
Blessed is the man who perseveres under trial, because when he has stood the test, he will receive the crown of life that God has promised to those who love him.

Lord, I do love You! I worship You in reverence and awe. Help me to persevere, to number my days, to take every opportunity to give You praise for the amazing things You have done and continue to do. Oh, that I will stand the test and receive all that You have promised.

I love the quote I read recently: "God didn't say it would be easy. He said it would be worth it." (source unknown)

Psalm 116:5-7
The LORD is gracious and righteous; our God is full of compassion.
The LORD protects the unwary; When I was brought low, he saved me.
Return to your rest, my soul, for the LORD has been good to you.

So many times I recall with great comfort when I really felt my soul
at rest because I reflected on Your goodness to me.

November 18th, 2012

This is the day You have made, a day You have ordained for
me to be present in my earthly body on this side of eternity.
It is good and You are good. I rejoice in Your goodness
to me. I take such great comfort in that You are sovereign
over the events in my life and in the world. As tempers
flare in the Middle East and we know things could get out
of control with man's decisions, we look to You knowing
nothing happens apart from your sovereign will.

I ask You for wisdom as I consider what to say in a letter to my
mother, thanking her for her generosity to my children. She
seems to be going downhill fast as I think about seeing her just
a month ago.

I humbly accept the Word You have planted in me and pray that
the words of my mouth and the meditations of my heart will be
pleasing in Your sight.

As Mike goes to Detroit today, I ask Your protection over him
and for clarity as he communicates Your love to this group of
students tomorrow morning.

I pray You grant them repentance leading to a knowledge of the truth, that each may experience the hope You offer in Christ.

November 19th, 2012

Thanksgiving week with lots of activities planned and a house full of family. I pray Your peace over all who enter our home, that we would honor You by our conversation and let You reign in our hearts. I love You, Lord, and thank You that we will have this family time together to make memories to treasure.

Ezekiel 39:7-8
I will make known my holy name among my people Israel. I will no longer let my holy name be profaned, and the nations will know that I the LORD am the Holy One in Israel. It is coming! It will surely take place, declares the Sovereign LORD. This is the day I have spoken of.

Lord, how I look forward to the day You have set when Your holy name will no longer be profaned. Knowing You have set a day on which from that point forward You will have said "enough" and will show Yourself holy beyond any doubt and will receive the honor and glory due You, never again to have Your name profaned by believers who forsake You (Ezekiel 20:27) and by unbelievers who mock You. Even so, come Lord Jesus.

Thank You for the reminder that mercy triumphs over judgment, but even Your tender, amazing mercy will end when the Day You have set for judgment arrives. Until then, thank You for Your mercies that are new each morning!

November 20th, 2012

Wisdom comes from You, and You freely give to all who ask You for it. The effect of wisdom is humility, as well as peace-loving. Your wisdom, seeing things and understanding from Your perspective, is full of mercy, considerate, sincere, and full of good fruit.

Psalm 118:29
Give thanks to the LORD, for he is good; his love endures forever.

November 21st, 2012

Giving thanks for the safe arrival of the Evans family late last night!

Tough getting to sleep last night with the nerves in my foot. I'm praying, begging for resolution there. Thank You that I know You understand and are merciful.

You, Lord, are full of compassion and mercy. Remind me to rest in that assurance today. Now, onward to live in the light of Your love and provision. For this day is the day You have made and ordained for me to live.

Your blessings be upon my mother as she is back in the hospital. And give Monica much-needed rest as she has got to be weary. Thank You that she can be here.

November 22nd, 2012

Thanksgiving Day
Looking forward to this day—having all our children, grandchildren, and spouses together—for time to share, making great memories, and sharing old memories. We have today as a gift from You. Help us all to cherish it, to really enjoy each other so that when we look back on this in years to come it will have special memories for everyone and fond remembrances of Your goodness to our family. I am grateful, eternally, for the new direction our family has taken because of Jesus. How different my legacy will be because of the new life I have that has now affected the next generations of my family forever! How great are You, God. How I rejoice in You and Your amazing grace.

November 23rd, 2012

Such a delightful day yesterday with the house full of family. Thank You for all of it. And the special time around the fire last night was such a treat for me. Having Monica here was an added blessing. I ask that You give her rest as she returns home.

1 Peter 1:24-25
All men are like grass, and all their glory is like the flowers of the field; the grass withers and the flowers fall, but the word of the Lord stands forever.

Psalm 119:48
I lift up my hands to your commands, which I love, and I meditate on your decrees.

Meditating on Your Word brings such comfort to my soul. So much of it has become so familiar through years of time reading and studying it. My confidence is sure, and my hope is unwavering. Thank You for Your faithfulness, of which I have come to know with increased awareness and appreciation. You are my life, my great reward.

November 26th, 2012

Monday after Thanksgiving. Everyone is home safely and full of memories of fun family times: gingerbread houses, decorating cookies, family pictures, backyard fire, food, football, little ones playing, hanging out. And having that article in the *Gwinnett Daily Post*—what an honor. Who could have planned that but You?

Visit with my mother at the hospital with the opportunity to pray for that man who coded was exciting. Seeing Molly and Maggie in action was pretty exciting!

My heart is full of gratitude as I reflect on Your goodness to me, Your kindness and favor. Thank You for every bit of it. I love You.

Psalm 119:89-90
Your word, O LORD, is eternal; it stands firm in the heavens. Your faithfulness continues through all generations; you established the earth, and it endures.

November 27th, 2012

As I read to my family around the fire on Thanksgiving night 1 Peter 1:3-9:

Praise be to the God and Father of our Lord Jesus Christ! In his great mercy he has given us new birth into a living hope through the resurrection of Jesus Christ from the dead, and into an inheritance that can never perish, spoil or fade—kept in heaven for you, who through faith are shielded by God's power until the coming of the salvation that is ready to be revealed in the last time. In this you greatly rejoice, though now for a little while you may have had to suffer grief in all kinds of trials. These have come so that your faith—of greater worth than gold, which perishes even though refined by fire—may be proved genuine and may result in praise, glory and honor when Jesus Christ is revealed. Though you have not seen him, you love him; and even though you do not see him now, you believe in him and are filled with an inexpressible and glorious joy, for you are receiving the goal of your faith, the salvation of your souls.

Thank You for Your great mercy that has given me new birth into a *living* hope and an imperishable inheritance in heaven as I am shielded by Your power and filled with inexpressible joy.

2 Peter 1:3
His divine power has given us everything we need for life and godliness through our knowledge of him who called us by his own glory and goodness.

God, Your divine power has given me everything I need for life and godliness through my knowledge of Him who called me for His own glory and goodness.

Psalm 119:111
Your statutes are my heritage forever; they are the joy of my heart.

November 28th, 2012

Oh, that I would honor You, God, the One who holds my life and all of my ways in Your hand.

Today, I return to Dr. Cool. Give him wisdom to provide for my situation, I ask. I'm not interested in spending time and money on empty efforts, but if he, in all his training halfway around the world has something that will improve my life, I'll take that as from Your hand of mercy.

Psalm 119:114
You are my refuge and my shield; I have put my hope in your word.

November 29th, 2012

I'm enjoying *A Severe Mercy*, the journey of faith, the love story, and interactions with C. S. Lewis by Sheldon Vanauken. The last day Vanauken and Lewis met for lunch, they talked about death and awakening after death. They thought their response would be, "Why, of course! Of course it's like this. How else could it have possibly been?" *(p. 125)*

I imagine the same or similar reaction except that I imagine it to be so much more amazing. My mind cannot imagine the depth of intense satisfaction never experienced on this side of eternity.

Then talking about their Oxford group and how they would say to each member as they left for the night, "Good bye, good night. Go under the mercy."

"Sleep under the protection, good night." *(p. 119)*

When Vanauken's wife inquired of C. S. Lewis about prayers to enlist the help of the Blessed Virgin, he responded, "If one's time for prayer was limited, the time one took for asking Mary's help was time one might be using for going directly to the Most High." *(p. 121)*

I remember my similar reaction to my Aunt Dorthy's request for prayer when we were lost while cross-country skiing as darkness approached. She announced we needed Mary's help. I remember saying, "Why not just go to our heavenly Father?"

Daniel 6:10
Three times a day [Daniel] got on his knees and prayed, giving thanks to his God.

It's all about thanking You Father, recognizing You as our Source and Sustainer and Provider and Protector. You are faithful to Your children.

2 Peter 3:13, 18
But in keeping with his promise we are looking forward to a new heaven and a new earth, the home of righteousness. . . . Grow in the grace and knowledge of our Lord and Savior Jesus Christ. To him be glory both now and forever! Amen.

Lord, I do want to continue to grow in grace and knowledge of You until the day I see You face to face. And then I'll say, "I thought I was in awe of You then." What a joyous day that will be. As I think of places in creation where I've been awed by Your work: the mountains in France, Colorado, Italy, the night sky at Camp Fitch, the full moon rising over the Atlantic, being in the middle of the Caribbean Ocean with no land in sight, sunsets over Lake Erie, Hawaii, the Scottish countryside, the west coast of Ireland and Wales. They all pale in comparison to what You have planned to show me, that place where Your glory dwells unveiled, where all is as it should be.

I give You thanks, Lord, countless blessing from Your hand and heart.

december 2012

December 1st, 2012

Thankful for a wonderful night's sleep! Didn't even wake up once! A couple hours with the empty nesters was fun and our first night out in a long time. Reading through some old journals, notes, and enjoying the reminders of what You were teaching me at other times in my life. The Falcons wives' study. The issue of faith is not so much whether we believe in God, but whether we believe the God we believe in. My relationship with God is purposeful, progressive, and personal. God is the Initiator, Enabler, and Sustainer.

December 5th, 2012

Back from a trip to Charlotte—our first outing since this battle
began. It was such a treat to be able to do this and fun to meet some
special people. Manti Te'o and his parents, Brian from the sports
information department at Notre Dame whose fourteen-year-old
adopted son is battling sarcoma. And to spend a little time with
Mike and Mary McNicholas. Thank You, Father, for Your traveling
mercies and the strength You provided for me to be able to do this.

In Hosea 2:19-20, You say You will betroth me to You forever in
righteousness and justice, in love and compassion and in faithfulness. Your vows are sure and I will acknowledge You forever. I can't
imagine what this looks like, but I know it will be amazing! You are
my awesome God!

Update #10
December 5th, 2012

Family and Friends,

I wanted to give y'all a quick update on the last few
days. We went to Charlotte on Monday for the Bronko
Nagurski Awards dinner. Mom did well on the three-
hour drive and then sitting at the table for three hours
during the awards ceremony. She met Manti Te'o at
a lunch earlier in the day. He saw her come in and he
immediately came over and helped her sit down and
got her leg situated on a pillow. She also received some
encouraging words from Coach Kelly.

On Tuesday, we drove from Charlotte directly to a doctor's appointment. We're still waiting on the results from the gene testing to see if any clinical trials are a match. The doctor was very impressed with her blood work. He said by looking at the numbers that she is recovering! What a huge encouragement!

We should know within the next ten days about the clinical trials and she'll be having another scan on her lungs at the beginning of January.

I was encouraged last week by a good friend. He said that this cancer is nothing that Mom can battle or that we can battle. It is God's battle. It is in His hands. There is no better place to be then to be in the hands of Jehovah-Rapha, the Lord who Heals.

Whatever befall . . .
Caleb

December 6th, 2012

Another good night's sleep. I am so grateful! Today I see Michelle and finally get the AFO (ankle-foot orthotic) for my leg. A couple busy days ahead.

I finished the book *A Severe Mercy* last night and finally realized what the meaning of severe mercy is. Your mercy is good, but it accomplishes whatever is necessary in each life. Sometimes we don't see it for what it is, thinking mercy is always gentle, but sometimes it needs to be severe to accomplish Your highest good. I do see that dimension in my life presently. My current battle has caused me to look at things so much differently. Many whose lives end abruptly may never see or understand this. By knowing life is going to end soon on this earth, my appreciation for each day is heightened; appreciation for time with loved ones is not taken for granted. Thank You for allowing me to see this.

And thank You for allowing me to witness in dimensions most never see—the work You have done to make my adult children who they are. Like experiencing personally Maggie's proficiency as an ICU nurse, seeing Molly and Maggie jump into action at the hospital when that man coded at St. Mary's, and Molly interacting on my behalf with the staff at Emory regarding my pain management. Katie administrating the coordination of our family pictures and her planning for the arrival of baby number three even though she doesn't have me to depend on. And of course Caleb, being thrown into the role of caregiver. How he firmly yet gently encouraged my physical therapy in the early days after surgery. I was so apprehensive about coming "home" versus going to an interim facility, yet You gave him the confidence that he could care for me as needed.

All this is a part of Your severe mercy in my life. Thank You for helping me understand that although living in the assurance of Your faithful and limitless mercy, sometimes it can feel like You've turned Your back, when actually I am experiencing the severe dimension of Your mercy either for my own sake or the sake of those close to me. You know what is necessary to accomplish what You desire in each person's life.

"If the dead do stay with us for a time, it might be allowed partly so that we may hang onto something of their reality." (p. 226) This was discussed between Lewis and Vanauken.

As C. S. Lewis wrote, "Circumstances have opened our eyes to see the sword which really hangs always over everyone." *(p. 227)*

He also wrote of his wife's "miraculous reprieve" as well as a "miraculous pardon," *(p. 228)* when her cancer came back.

I thank You that Monica and I were able to take so many trips in memory of our dear daddy and to see so clearly in each place a special "something" that really spoke to us of his presence—none so clearly to me as the tenth anniversary of his death while we were dining in the Paris restaurant on the eve of what would have been his 90th birthday and the first competition in my adult career. When the flower salesman walked to our table and presented me with a yellow rose, no charge: Why me? There were six of us seated there—Caleb, Crista, Zoe, Dan, along with Monica and me—all witnesses to this amazing act. My only thought was, "This is from Dad." Of course, by Your hand, a sweet memory of Your involvement in the details of my life. You certainly didn't have to do that. By it, You confirmed again to me Your assurance that You have my earthly dad firmly in Your care, and the absolute joy I experienced on the ice on his 90th birthday was a confirmation of taking his advice: "Live it up." It certainly would have delighted him.

December 7th, 2012

Between Michelle Polk and Dr. Cool, I am getting treatments that are unconventional, so what is conventional is not always the best. Reports from my blood work made the doctor say, "It looks like you're recovering." I guess that means it's not what he expected. All I know is that I feel good. This battle is Yours and I will live every day that You have ordained for me to live. I ask that You help me appreciate each day and every encounter that You provide.

Psalm 125:1-2
Those who trust in the LORD *are like Mount Zion, which cannot be shaken but endures forever. As the mountains surround Jerusalem, so the* LORD *surrounds his people both now and forevermore.*

Thank You, Father, that these things I know, both because Your Word says so and because I have experienced it so faithfully in my life. You indeed surround me with Your love and protection. I am never out of Your sight. I rest in Your promises. You are my faithful God.

December 8th, 2012

Jude 1:21, 24-25
Keep yourselves in God's love as you wait for the mercy of our Lord Jesus Christ to bring you to eternal life. . . . To him who is able to keep you from falling and to present you before his glorious presence without fault and with great joy—to the only God our Savior be glory, majesty, power and authority, through Jesus Christ our Lord, before all ages, now and forevermore! Amen.

Yes Lord, You and only You are able to keep me from falling and to present me before Your glorious presence without fault and with great joy. How I thank You for that reminder today. I am able to do all things through Christ who is my strength!

And there is mercy again in Jude 1:21, as I wait for the mercy of Jesus to bring me to eternal life. Yes, sometimes Your mercy is severe, but it is always what You need it to be and adequate for my need. Thank You that I can trust You to be merciful, full of mercy toward me. You desire mercy, not sacrifice, and mercy triumphs over judgment. Open my eyes to Your mercy today.

December 9th, 2012

Thank You for the delightful time with Kathy and Dave Straughan yesterday. It felt almost "normal" to be going out to a friend's for a meal. It was such a treat for me and a gift from You. As we were driving, I was thinking about just how good I felt, except for my leg of course. If this is Your miraculous reprieve, I'll take it.

I awake to a day of sun as the fog is lifting. I ask that You give me the strength to get these ministry letters done and ask Your blessing on the request there in.

Lord, You proclaim in Joel 2:12-14:
"Even now," declares the LORD, "return to me with all your heart, with fasting and weeping and mourning." Rend your heart and not your garments. Return to the LORD your God, for he is gracious and compassionate, slow to anger and abounding in love, and he relents from sending calamity. Who knows? He may turn and have pity and leave behind a blessing.

Your desire is my inward reaction not what others see. Your character is gracious and compassionate, always patient and merciful and slow to anger. Even so, Lord, the Day is coming when You will finally say, "Enough!" and so it will be that day when Your mercy, severe and tender, will have reached its end and every knee will bend to Your authority absolutely.

Thinking about this new baby due to arrive shortly and trusting You for safe arrival and timing. What a wonderful gift, no better. And that who he/she is an absolute surprise, thank You. This baby was known by You and his/her days known by You before we knew of my situation and what a gift to our family that You ordained this blessing. You have left Your blessing in the midst of sadness in our family.

Maybe they should name "him" Ephraim, "God has blessed me in the land of my suffering." Isn't that the truth though, Lord? Despite our grief, no matter the situation, we always have Your blessings. As Your children were in Babylonian captivity, You instructed them to pray for Babylonian prosperity so they would experience blessing in the land of captivity. Even though I am "captive" to the conditions from my surgery, I am experiencing Your blessing daily in so many ways!

Ephraim: *"It is because God has made me fruitful in the land of my suffering"* (Genesis 41:12).

I do pray You make me fruitful in this time of my "suffering."

December 11th, 2012

Reflections: praying for wisdom for Mary-Jo as she decides what option to choose going forward. Thank You that You give wisdom when we ask. Let my counsel be from You when I have opportunity to speak.

Last night was so special at the Christmas party. Thank You for the gift of friends—brothers and sisters in Christ—who are surrounding me with prayer and genuine concern. I pray it was a blessing for Caleb as he experienced the words and actions of dear friends of his parents.

Bless Jeff and Gregg, Mark and Susie, Tim and Barb, Paul and Kym, John and Kathryn, JB and Laurie, Sunny and Todd, Ernie and his wife. My illness has impacted so many, brought them to their knees. I ask that what they see in me of You would be an encouragement to them in their faith. To You be the glory in all.

Psalm 130: 5, 7
I wait for the LORD, my soul waits, and in his word I put my hope. . . .
for with the LORD is unfailing love and with him is full redemption.

December 11ᵗʰ, 2012, Evening

So fun to Skype with Katie, Rody, and Anna Kate. Thankful for this technology, wearing Santa masks. We had fun ho-ho-ho-ing.

So, another "wow" day as we went to Athens to shop and stopped to see Mother. I was surprised that Kevin was there, but came to realize he made the trip to deliver a check for me. She said since I was feeling so good maybe I'd like to take a trip with Mike or maybe everyone, and I wouldn't have to worry about money. I told her about my identification with the writer who talked about Jesus and the night before he died, how He just wanted to bless those He loved, and that's how I feel. She seemed to perk up just having me there. Again, I can't imagine being a parent of a child who is dying; surely I'd want to do whatever I could to make sure the child was happy and cared for.

December 12ᵗʰ, 2012

Sweet Kylie turns fifteen today—amazing. So many dear memories of this special child who has taught me how to be a Grandma.

The first hours, the first days and weeks, the craft project making those Christmas hankies with her hand and footprints, just watching her sleep, caring for her while Molly was in class in the early weeks, being amazed by this baby—my baby's baby! How she loved the cow, just stared at it. Her first steps at our house, the reaction to her daddy's shushing, how she wanted to dress like Jason. Camp Fitch memories: the horse, rocks at the beach, so much fun through the years and more recently the travel. Oberstdorf in 2011 and then Paris this year! I'm so grateful for the glimpses of who she is becoming—her presentation after her trip to Ethiopia. It's obvious that You have captured her heart and I just ask that You continue to mold her and protect her and give her Your eyes to see the world—the people You have made—as You see them. Thank You for the courage that is already evident, to live for You in the face of challenging circumstances. I couldn't have asked for a better firstborn grandchild, one who continues to amaze me with her life and giftedness. We celebrate her today. Give her assurance of Your love for her. The journey has just begun.

July 27ᵗʰ, 1999

My precious Lord, how I treasure You! Thank You for these few special days with Kylie. She is a reminder to me of Your faithfulness. She is so wide-eyed and dependent, exactly how I want to be with You—ever learning, ever trusting.

Jeremiah 17:7-8
Blessed is the man who trusts in the LORD, whose confidence is in him. He will be like a tree planted by water. . . It does not fear when heat comes. . . It has no worries in a year of drought.

A tree planted by water has the life source it needs to grow and stay healthy. Regardless of extremes of conditions, it survives. Help me to renew my confidence in You, Lord, and to grow deep roots of trust. Even in times of drought I will stand firm for the right relationship I have with You.

December 12th, 2001

We celebrate Kylie's 4th birthday today and bring her before You with grateful praise. What a sweet blessing she is. Continue to protect her tender spirit as You teach her about Yourself. When I remember her sitting on my dad's lap, holding his hand, wiping his face, sharing his cookies, I am reminded of the truth of Your Word—that the purposes of Your heart stand firm through all generations. Your love transcends the ages and I have beheld Your goodness in the land of the living.

December 12th, 2004

Happy Birthday Kylie, seven years old, just talked with her by phone, she told me she got a new Bible, one that doesn't have pictures, just a couple, just Your Word! Thank You again for her and all the joy she has brought into my life. I praise You for leading her to Yourself just this year, baptized, identified with You! I think about my grandma Gladys, probably about the same age and responding to you then. I thank You for my great grandma, Rose Secoy Moore, who mothered only nine years, yet gave her daughter Gladys the most important gift, faith. And that I had the opportunity 70 plus years later to reintroduce her to an "old friend", Jesus.

Your ways are indeed higher than mine. I am blessed!

December 13th, 2012

My heart is burdened for my mother today, for her health as she continues in the rehab facility. Just wondering if she's given up? Lord, You know her condition; she has to be discouraged with her own health situation, but then to be burdened with her concern for me. How did I not see this? I pray for opportunities to assure her that I am okay. I ask that You bring her comfort through ways only You can today.

When I think of my emotions that come from time invested with You in Your Word, seeing You act on my behalf, coming to understand grace and mercy, knowing You in the day-to-day as well as entrusting to You my eternal security, all that You have provided and having the assurance that You are who You say You are, that You are faithful and able, kind and merciful, compassionate and trustworthy—my confidence is in You—but my faith is not blind, because You have opened my eyes to see. This is me, Christ in me, the hope of glory, so much greater than any award this world provides.

But what confidence does my mother have as she sees her life deteriorating?

I remember my dad's doubts and I'd reassure him of Your promises in Your Word, and he'd say, "Are you sure?" And, "I wish I would have studied more." His heart was so tender and teachable and trusting. But here is a woman who has always been confident in her view and opinions who now faces losing control. Lord, You know her heart. Show Your mercy to her at this time. Help me to do and say what I can that will bring comfort to her. Open her eyes that she may see You and trust in Your unending love with humility and faith.

Revelation 4:11
You are worthy, our Lord and God, to receive glory and honor and power, for you created all things, and by your will they were created and have their being.

December 9th, 2001

It is pleasing to You when I *"put my religion into practice by caring for my own family and so repaying their parents and grandparents."* (1 Timothy 5:4) If I was doing this to receive gratitude or to cause a change, it hasn't happened. You alone know how my heart hurts when I consider the bankrupt estate of my mother's heart. You alone know what's going on in her mind and heart. I pray that You crush her heart of stone and replace it with a heart to seek You, Your truth—not as she perceives from natural reasoning. I pray that she would recognize her own need for Your mercy and not be so concerned with everyone else. Allow me to continue to be a faithful vessel of Your compassion and not to rely on my own reserves, that my actions and attitudes would be pleasing to You and bring You Glory. My honor depends on You!

March 9th, 1983

It would have been so easy to be anxious today, but I kept claiming Your Word as truth. Isaiah 55:10-11. The morning meeting went the smoothest ever. I realized that so many are praying. My first thought as I greeted mother for our trip to the Kahkwa Club was, "She's really on edge." And boy was she. Lord, You answered so many prayers today. It was so inspiring—my fearlessness to proclaim Your gospel of love! Now I know Mother has heard, her ears were open. Please, Lord, don't let her rest until she's found answers. Her comments were positive and I don't know that You made a convert, or whatever You call it, of me, but it was certainly time well spent.

December 14th, 2012

You alone are worthy, Lord! You alone are Sovereign. *"Worthy is the Lamb, who was slain, to receive power and wealth and wisdom and strength and honor and glory and praise!" (Revelation 5:12).* You are worthy of it all Jesus.

I really do love Psalm 33, to meditate on its richness, what it says about You.

Thank You that Mike is home, fall schedule complete. As we look forward to the weeks ahead, I ask that You guide our conversations. Give healing to our bodies and peace to our minds and hearts. So much to look forward to—a new baby, time with Maggie and Jeff, time at the beach with the Evans family.

December 15th, 2012

Full day yesterday. Continuing to ask for guidance and peace for Mary Jo as she makes a decision about her treatment. All I can give her is confidence that You will give her wisdom. My heart aches for her but I know You are faithful.

And how my heart aches for these families in Connecticut who were torn apart by the actions of one man, killing twenty children and six adults in an elementary school. I know as I've read *The Story of Civilization* that there is indeed nothing new under the sun. Man's heart is bent toward evil, but we have come to expect respect and civility, yet evil lurks in our midst. Have mercy, Lord. Please comfort these as only You can.

Back to my day—the doctor visit and seeing the x-ray, amazing medicine, most amazing God! Then out to dinner at Moe's and actually walking around a store. Such a treat.

Off to Dr. Cool's party and then to visit Rose. You are indeed gracious, Lord, to give me strength and energy to do all these things.

December 16th, 2012

Psalm 33:1
Sing joyfully to the LORD, you righteous: it is fitting for the upright to praise you.

Looking forward to going to GCC this morning. Thankful for all the fun yesterday—the party at Dr. Cool's, trip to Athens, seeing Mother and sister Sheila, the live nativity program at a local church, and seeing the lights to music on the house in Jefferson. It's all good.

Micah 6:8
He has showed you, O man, what is good. And what does the LORD require of you? To act justly and to love mercy and to walk humbly with your God.

Other treasures from the prophet Micah.

Micah 7:7 (regardless of how bad it gets)
But as for me, I watch in hope for the LORD, I wait for God my Savior; my God will hear me.

Micah 7:18-20
Who is a God like you, who pardons sin and forgives the transgression of the remnant of his inheritance? You do not stay angry forever but delight to show mercy. You will again have compassion on us; you will tread our sins underfoot and hurl all our iniquities into the depths of the sea. You will be true to Jacob, and show mercy to Abraham, as you pledged on oath to our fathers in days long ago.

Proverbs 30:5
Every word of God is flawless; he is a shield to those who take refuge in him.

How I love Your Word, Lord. Thank You for giving me a hunger and thirst for it. You are being faithful to produce peace in my heart as the effect of time in Your Word produces. You are indeed good; let me proclaim Your goodness.

December 17th, 2012

Nahum 1:3, 7
The LORD is slow to anger and great in power; the LORD will not leave the guilty unpunished. His way is in the whirlwind and the storm, and clouds are the dust of his feet. . . . The LORD is good, a refuge in times of trouble. He cares for those who trust in him.

Thank You for being my refuge, Lord. You have indeed been faithful. May all who see me know that You are my faithful God.

I am so happy for Monica as her girls arrive today. Give them cherished moments together as they just enjoy each other. From California to Morocco—despite the distance, You bring them together to have times of blessing and encouragement.

December 18th, 2012

Yesterday, was a milestone as I drove myself to therapy. Because of scheduling conflicts I needed a ride to therapy and then it dawned on me—I can drive. I didn't know if it would work, but after practicing the logistics, it was a go. All went well. Thank You for small favors!

Habakkuk 3:17-19
Though the fig tree does not bud and there are no grapes on the vines, though the olive crop fails and the fields produce no food, though there are no sheep in the pen and no cattle in the stalls, yet I will rejoice in the LORD, *I will be joyful in God my Savior. The sovereign* LORD *is my strength; he makes my feet like the feet of a deer, he enables me to go on the heights.*

No matter what happens or the desperation of the times, I will be joyful in You, my Savior. You are my strength! You have been put to the test and have proved Your faithfulness to me over and over.

I couldn't help but think, and it was so hard to keep my mouth shut, when Sister Sheila was talking about someone ready to "go." How they were looking forward to seeing their husband and parents again. I just wanted to shout, "But what about Jesus? The One who died for you?"

Yes, it will be wonderful to have a great cloud of witnesses including so many loved ones, but they are just a sweet addition to the unimaginable joy of seeing Your face, of bowing before You in inexpressible humble gratitude and overwhelming praise. It's all about being in Your presence—that's how I see it. I know my eye has not seen (and I have seen some amazing things in Your creation), my ears have not heard, nor has entered into my imagination what You have planned for me. Whenever that day comes.

December 19th, 2012

Psalm 138:7-8
Though I walk in the midst of trouble, you preserve my life . . . with your right hand you save me. The LORD will fulfill [his purpose] for me; your love, O LORD, endures forever—do not abandon the works of your hands.

Thank You, Lord, for the faithful prayers of Your people on my behalf. I am so grateful for each one. I pray Your blessing on all who remember me before Your throne!

December 20th, 2012

Reflecting on Zephaniah, I am reminded that the day is coming when every person will bend their knees to You and declare You as the awesome God—every single one! Your name and honor will no longer be profaned. And never again will You be dishonored. How I long for that day.

Retirement party for Jim Kelly last night, and at 78, he's finally going to take some time off—maybe. I do pray You give him and

Bobbie some rest and enjoyment in this season. It was so good to meet Chris and see he's doing well—an answer to many prayers. And that Jim would recognize Mike out of all those people shows he understands the real importance in life. How any parent or grandparent would give all they could to help a child they love. And to see this matters to Jim above anything else he could point to.

Today's Psalm is Psalm 139. Love it!

Psalm 139:13-18
For you created my inmost being; you knit me together in my mother's womb. I praise you because I am fearfully and wonderfully made; your works are wonderful, I know that full well. My frame was not hidden from you when I was made in the secret place. When I was woven together in the depths of the earth, your eyes saw my unformed body. All the days ordained for me were written in your book before one of them came to be. How precious to me are your thoughts, O God! How vast is the sum of them! Were I to count them, they would outnumber the grains of sand. When I awake, I am still with you.... Search me, O God, and know my heart; test me and know my anxious thoughts. See if there is any offensive way in me, and lead me in the way everlasting.

No one knows me like You do, Lord. Even I do not understand myself. Knowing You know me and those I love so completely. I know I can trust You to be their sovereign Lord. I do rest in this confidence. Now, onward to the day ahead. Thank You for getting Maggie safely to North Carolina ahead of the big storm.

December 22nd, 2012

Thank You for the safe arrival yesterday of David McCoy Barnett— Coy as he will be called. It was such a wonderful family time just being together to celebrate and welcome this new life. And my favorite thing—just holding and rocking a baby. I treasured looking at his sweet face and felt quite emotional thinking I may never hear him call me grandma, but I prayed he would come to know You and spend eternity as part of our forever family.

Thank You, too, for Katie's birthing experience—just four hours of labor. You didn't have to be so kind, but You were!

How I treasure the look of complete joy when Rody entered the room and first saw his new brother. His eyes lit up and his smile was so genuine—not a hint of concern or doubt.

Then Anna Kate—being overwhelmed with the whole scene. The hospital, mommy in bed, baby crying, all the family . . . but she warmed up over time. How she ran to give me a hug before I left. So sweet and another of my treasures.

Bless this family I pray as they grow together.
12-21-12
12:27 p.m.
8 lbs. 11oz.

December 27th, 2012

The actions of people or nations are hard to understand. I must remember that until Your Word is fulfilled, You continue to put into the ears of them things that will accomplish Your purposes.

You are in control—sovereign—even when it doesn't appear that You are. Thank You, Lord, that I can trust You to accomplish Your purposes in every generation.

December 28th, 2012

Zechariah 12:1
The LORD, who stretches out the heavens, who lays the foundation of the earth, and who forms the spirit of a man within him, declares . . .

Yes, Lord. Whatever You declare so, it is. You hold absolute power and authority over men and nations. It has always been as You declare, and You are trustworthy to complete as You have promised.

Thank You for making Yourself known to me. Thank You for holding my life and welfare in Your hand. I have been so blessed with the outpouring of petitions for my health and healing that have been brought before Your throne. Thank You for each person, each prayer, and each expression of concern.

I really feel so good and healthy and have been able to enjoy so many things these last couple months. Thank You for Monte and Phyllis and the friends they have been. I ask Your protection over Courtney as she carries this new life. Bless their time together in the mountains these next few days. It was so good to see them yesterday!

Psalm 147:3-7, 10-11
He heals the brokenhearted and binds up their wounds. He determines the number of the stars and calls them each by name. Great is our Lord and mighty in power; his understanding has no limit. The LORD sustains the humble but casts the wicked to the ground. Sing to the LORD with thanksgiving; make music to our God on the harp. . . . His pleasure is not in the strength of the horse, nor his delight in the legs of man; the LORD delights in those who fear him, who put their hope in his unfailing love.

I do put my hope in Your unfailing love, Lord. You have been faithful in all Your ways, and as I look over my life, I see the hand of Your faithfulness throughout it so very clearly. Faithfulness is Your essence. Thank You for opening my eyes to see!

December 31st, 2012

Arrived at Fripp Island yesterday for a few days of beach time. Awoke to a beautiful sunny day and almost a full moon over the Atlantic last night. Fun gazing into the heavens with the kids and grandkids, with Katie giving instructions on the stars. Thank You for these times with all the grandkids. Fun "matching" earrings with Anna Kate this morning and holding baby Coy last night. I am so rich! Bless Mike and Mary for their willingness to share this place with us.

Even the new dog "Champ" is enjoying the festivities.

Malachi 1:11
My name will be great among the nations, from the rising to the setting of the sun.

You are not wearied by earnest prayers, pleading on behalf of loved ones for Your actions, or repetitive praise. You are wearied by words of compromise, relativism, and questions of Your sovereignty. Man throughout history has wearied You by their words of unbelief about who You say You are, of what You say is true. How I long for the day when there will be no more of this, when You receive the praise due You, when Your name is great among the nations without question, from the rising of the sun . . .

December 31ˢᵗ, 2011

The day dawns on the last day of 2011, and my heart overflows with gratitude. Your faithfulness to me throughout another calendar year with so many blessings to reflect on and sweet memories.

Thank You for the one month of preparation for the French Cup and the wonderful time in Paris. Finding out I really enjoyed skating in competition, the sweet gift of the yellow rose, time with Caleb, the 10th anniversary of Dad's home going and skating on his 90th birthday—really special. How the Germany trip worked out with Kylie and Katie, Monica and her girls—seven of us for a week in Oberstdorf! Wow. Westfield and Camp Fitch. Trips to Vermont, Connecticut, Arkansas, Texas, and then to Dublin. And a new son-in-law! Rose actually came to watch Monica and me skate at the Peach Open. Surviving the kidney infection.

I ask that You continue to teach me to listen—to really hear—what You are saying to me through Your Word and that my intentions would always be to have my heart set to honor You and Your name in my "world."

january 2013

January 1st, 2013

And the sun rises over the Atlantic. I praise You! At the start of another calendar year, in the beginning all praise and honor goes to You. As I spend these few days with my family enjoying Your goodness to me, I am aware of Your presence, Your sovereignty. A few months ago I was feeling so sick and the outlook was dismal, yet I was looking forward to all You have planned. How I feel so good and I am grateful for each day, even though I have physical limitations. Whatever Your plans are for me, I know they are good. You alone hold my earthly and eternal future, and I trust You. So many have prayed and continue to pray for me, yet You are not wearied by the repetitive requests on my behalf. So as this new year begins, I entrust myself to Your care and know You are worthy of all my praise.

January 1ˢᵗ, 2012

It looks like a couple weeks of calm before the traveling and business starts. Lord, I know whatever You have
planned for my 2012, it is good, because You are good!
Bless my children, I pray, each in a good place with You,
and my mother as she continues to heal and hope for
better days. Thank You for Mike. Keep him focused and
set to follow You wherever You lead him.

January 2ⁿᵈ, 2012

Help me remember. Your Word is such a comfort
and has become my constant guide. You have been so
faithful to do as You say, because You always are who
You are. There is no shadow of turning with You.

January 2ⁿᵈ, 2013

As I watch the waves crash to the shore, another day at the beach
dawns. I enjoyed the moonlit sky as I got up late last night.
Everything of creation that my eyes see I have great wonder for.
You are my God and created all my eyes see. I stand in awe of You.

That I am able to take the steps up and down at the beach house
is amazing. I thought for sure that I'd have to be carried, yet with
Caleb's encouragement and confidence, I gave it a try. Kylie driving
the golf cart was a treat too.

Give Katie some rest and refreshment today as Randy goes back to
work and she continues on her journey as a mother of three. I'm so

thankful for the time I get to hold little Coy and just hang out with him. Such a treat!

January 3rd, 2012

I remember that flight attendant saying in my ear as he passed by my seat—just "John 16:33" was all he said. I wonder if he saw the weariness on my face. Bless him today as he was such a blessing to me probably ten years ago. The value of Your Word, an encouragement at all times and in all places.

April 2nd, 2001

Yesterday, on the plane from Raleigh, as I started working on my study, the voice of the steward in my ear saying, "John 16:33." Where did that come from and why? Jesus said:

"I have told you these things, so that in me you may have peace. In this world you will have trouble. But take heart! I have overcome the world." (John 16:33).

January 4th, 2013

Beautiful sunrise over the Atlantic. Your faithful reminder of another day as it should be in Your sovereignty.

Enjoyed some special time with Kylie and Kaitlyn last night and a few moments of snuggling with Molly. I ask that You continue to grow and protect them, as I trust You know what is best for each.

Let us enjoy this day You have given us in South Carolina, in Your goodness.

January 5th, 2013

As I watch another beautiful sunrise, my thoughts go to Psalm 33:6, *By the word of the LORD were the heavens made, their starry host by the breath of our mouth.* You spoke and it came to be. You commanded and it stood firm. Talk about "unfailing." You are amazing and I am in awe of You. One more beautiful day on this side of eternity.

Unfailing love.

Psalm 33:5
The earth is full of your unfailing love.

Psalm 33:18
The eyes of the LORD are on those who fear him, on those whose hope is in his unfailing love.

Psalm 33:22
May your unfailing love rest upon us, O LORD, even as we put our hope in you.

Whatever I need to adjust my perspective, Psalm 33 is a great place to camp!

Yesterday's joys ended with reading two books to Kasen, *There Was a Coyote* and *10 Little Hermit Crabs*. Such fun!

The sunset on the beach, Kaitlyn painting my toes, shopping with the girls and Karson, singing sunshine songs, and Kylie asking questions from the chat pack, all treasured memories.

January 7th, 2013

Game Day is finally here. Notre Dame plays Alabama tonight for the National Championship. I just pray no one gets hurt.

Reflecting on such a fun week with family at the beach in Your beautiful creation!

Things are not looking good for Rose's improvement and her return to Highland Hill. This has been such a rapid decline. I realize that if she's moved to North Carolina, I may never see her again. How can this be? Help me to find the words when I do see her, to make it count—words of truth yet assuring her that I'm okay.

Genesis 18:12, 14
Sarah laughed to herself as she thought, "After I am worn out and my master is old, will I now have this pleasure? . . . . Is anything too hard for the LORD?"

Lord, I know *nothing* is too hard for You, for You raised Jesus from the dead. Thank You that I know with confidence that You are able. When the experts express their confident, educated opinions, it can never trump Your will. For You are the all-powerful sovereign God in whom I trust.

Matthew 6:7-8
Jesus on the Mount
"When you pray, do not keep on babbling like pagans, for they think they will be heard because of their many words. Do not be like them, for your Father knows what you need before you ask him."

You are my help. You know what I need before I ever ask and even when I can't put into words what I am asking for, You meet my needs out of Your love.

Remind me to use the words of Jesus, "Our Father." Fifty-two words. And I know You don't hear me because of the number of words. You hear my heart even when there aren't even words coming from my mouth.

Thank You for this reminder today.

January 10th, 2013

Everything God requires, He provides.

Thought of this yesterday as I read about Abraham and Isaac. Thank You for the teaching of Russ McKnight and how this principle has stuck with me through the years.

So, my heart breaks at the news of Mary Jo's cancer in her liver. Lord, she is only 43, and it looks like such a desperate battle ahead. I pray You give her wisdom to make the best decision going forward, and give her strength physically and mentally to carry on strong. Help me to be an encourager in any way I can. I bring her before You and ask that You heal her. I will keep asking.

How I have loved reading Ken Hutcherson's take on Matthew 15, the Canaanite woman, desperation!

From a human perspective Jesus walked right by her, ignoring her, and not caring about her. From an eternal perspective, God is sovereign. He was saying, "Follow Me, keep asking. You're not going to believe how strong you are. Your daughter is going to be fine. And so are you."

We are never told about her again, but she had to be forever changed, telling all her friends about Jesus and facing the rest of her life with enormous confidence and trust in God.

Tough times teach us what we know in our heads, and it becomes implanted in our hearts. All things work together for good if you love Jesus.

Proverbs 3:5-6
Trust in the LORD with all your heart and lean not on your own understanding; in all your ways acknowledge him, and he will make your paths straight.

Any time I lean on my own understanding, things can look very confusing. Your ways are so much higher than mine. I do acknowledge You as my sovereign Lord, and I know You will make all my paths straight according to Your will.

Make Mary Jo's path straight.

January 11th, 2013

Caleb is off to Minnesota. It's hard to believe his time here is coming to an end. I do ask that You guide his steps and keep him safe. Thank You for Your abundant promise and unfailing love, for lessons learned and the foundation of faith. As he travels his unique path, may he continue to honor You in all his actions.

Proverbs 3:7-8
Do not be wise in your own eyes; fear the LORD and shun evil. This will bring health to your body and nourishment to your bones.

Charles Spurgeon on heaven: "To come to Thee is to come home from exile." (source unknown)

January 12ᵗʰ, 2013

In the morning I lay my requests before You and wait in
expectation for Your answers. I bring You Angie Bundy and Mary Jo
with their health issues, and Michelle with her concerns for Maddy
and Michala, and Kevin and Anne with Martin's future. So many
heavy concerns people are dealing with, and I know You are the
only source of help. So I bring these to You knowing that is the very
best I can do for those I care about. I can offer encouragement and
support and the confidence that I have because I have learned to
trust You.

Psalm 10:17
You hear, O LORD, the desires of the afflicted; you encourage them, and
you listen to their cry.

January 13ᵗʰ, 2004

Thank You for the gift of my great grandmother's
(Rose Secoy Moore) Bible that my mother has had for
years! I'm looking forward to typing out the verses she
has marked and know that I will be blessed as this will
give me a picture of her faith in You. What a treasure!

January 14ᵗʰ, 2013

So much talk of return on investment, and Your Word says in
Proverbs 3:13-15, *Blessed is the man who finds wisdom, the man who*
gains understanding, for she is more profitable than silver and yields
better returns than gold. She is more precious than rubies; nothing you
desire can compare with her.

Money has no value when it comes to purchasing eternity, nothing that will last. Storing up for security has no lasting value— only wisdom gained from You is true blessing. When I see Your face and realize You are so much more than I ever imagined, I will realize in fact the blessings You have provided. Here and now, I feel so blessed by what I have learned from You through time in Your Word and with Your people.

January 15th, 2013

Just thinking how Jacob was returning to Canaan after being away twenty years, and Isaac was still alive. He had worked so hard and it wasn't easy. He survived the encounter with Laban his father-in-law, and then Jacob calls out Laban. Genesis 31:36-44.

At least he recognized that You—the God of Abraham—had been with him and saw the hardship he endured and the toil his hands experienced. You kept Laban from harming him. Then on to meet Esau, who was coming to meet him with four hundred of his men. It had been twenty years. Had Esau continued to console himself with thoughts of revenge? Or had the twenty years added perspective?

As Jacob prayed, *"I am unworthy of all the kindness and faithfulness you have shown your servant" (Genesis 32:10).* No kidding! Are any of us worthy? Jacob certainly had to remember what he had done, with his mother's encouragement, before he'd left Cannon twenty years prior.

The fear of his father Isaac?

"If you can't fly, then run
If you can't run, then walk

If you can't walk, then crawl
You have to keep moving forward." —Martin Luther King, Jr.
(source unknown)

January 16th, 2013

Moving forward. Continuing to climb the stairs and do some
walking with the cane. It's all good.

Praying for Mary Jo today as she meets with another doctor. Reveal
Your best plan to her, and I ask, remind her to come to You when
she's weary and burdened. You will give her rest. Your yoke is easy
and Your burden is light.

Matthew 11:28-30
*"Come to me, all you who are weary and burdened, and I will give you
rest. Take my yoke upon you and learn from me, for I am gentle and
humble in heart, and you will find rest for your souls. For my yoke is easy
and my burden is light."*

How often I need this simple reminder. Your yoke is easy and Your
burden is light. There is no reason for me to ever be weary and
burdened. Thank You for reminding me today. Help me to use these
words of encouragement for others.

January 17th, 2013

Another day dawns. Grateful for sleep and feeling good!

Jesus, You desire mercy not sacrifice. Keep teaching me the meaning
of this, I pray.

January 19th, 2013

Psalm 18:30
As for God, his way is perfect; the word of the LORD is flawless. He is a shield for all who take refuge in him.

Thank You for the sweet time with Katie and Coy this weekend. It is pure joy to hold a baby, especially this one. You know how I'd love to see him grow up, so I pray You open his ears and eyes and mind to hear and see and understand the truth of who You are—and that he respond in repentance and faith.

Bless You, Lord. My soul rejoices in who You are.

January 22nd, 2013

Grateful for today. Praying for Martin as he adjusts to his new school.

And thankful for yesterday's surprise visit from Bonnie and Rich McGeorge. I do pray for him, and for her, that You make yourself known to them. If not already. What a rough road! Our lives crossed at that crucial time when our marriages were new, and our friendship grew through childbirth and football.

Reading about Joseph revealing himself to his brothers in Egypt and realizing You had a plan in all that happened to him. You protected him, and You gave him a position of power where he could bless and provide for his entire family.

You are my God as well, and I know that You are providing for and protecting me, and that You are and will bless my loved ones through what You are doing in my life.

I'm so thankful that Monica is able to spend time here. Your goodness to us is amazing!

January 23rd, 2013

Lord, I need wisdom to decide what to do going forward. I feel so good, yet a decision needs to be made about participating in this study in Ohio—about having a scan here to see what's going on inside me now.

Moving forward with plans for a cruise. If it is a wise thing, and where, and if Kylie and Kaitlyn can go with us.

Genesis 46:3-4
Jacob is on his way to Egypt to see Joseph whom he thought had been killed many years prior. He stopped to sacrifice to You, and You then spoke to him in a vision:

"Do not be afraid . . . and Joseph's own hand will close your eyes."

I think, how tender of You to meet Jacob at his deepest need in this personal way. You do indeed heal every hurt. For so many years, Jacob had been grieving and fearful of losing Benjamin as well. I can't imagine the family gathering where the others were living with the truth of what had happened to Joseph. That is so true of my life as well, in that I can't see the whole picture. I don't understand why Brian "left" our family, and I don't know why we felt so on edge through the years with Mother—but You know how each of us is wired. You honored Dad's wish that strangers not orchestrate his final symphony. How sweet it was for Monica and me to be with him as he entered Your presence. You knew his heart's desire, and You blessed him and us by sweetly allowing, planning, his exit to be what it was.

January 24th, 2013

So sad yesterday as Monica, Kevin, and I visited Rose. She seemed so distant, as I tried to engage her in conversation. Only You, Lord, know the length of her days. I just pray that You make Yourself real to her where she is. When given to fear, remind her of Your presence. I know how prone to worry she is, so I ask that You guard her heart and remind her that she has children who are caring for her the best we can. Thank You for Your tender-hearted mercies.

January 26th, 2013

Lord, You know the concerns on my heart. I come to You this morning and lay my requests before You and wait in expectation for Your answers. There are so many distractions, but I know You are my solid rock.

Thank You for Dr. Dave, his perspective and his caring. Help Mike to consider all his options and make wise decisions.

Planning this cruise has been fun if it's to be. I know You will take care of the details.

I know Your unfailing love is able to comfort Cecelia's husband as he grieves the loss of his wife and daughters. I can't imagine his pain, but I trust You to meet him where he is and strengthen him. May all who memorialize them today be blessed by their lives and be given hope from Your Word. In the days, months, and years ahead, please be a constant companion to this man that he may find You sufficient for his every need.

January 27th, 2013

I do rejoice in You—my Lord, my Redeemer and King.

Thank You for the reminder today of the importance of little ones to You.

Matthew 18:10
"See that you do not look down on one of these little ones. For I tell you that their angels in heaven always see the face of my Father in heaven."

Then the story about the one hundred sheep. One wanders, and You're happier about the sheep being found.

Matthew 18:14
"In the same way your Father in heaven is not willing that any of these little ones should be lost."

How special little ones are to You. Help me to enjoy the little ones You've put in my family during the times I have with them, knowing they are near to Your heart and their angels always see Your face.

Give us guidance as we plan for this cruise next month. It looks like it will be such fun if Kylie and Kaitlyn can be with us too.

January 28th, 2013

Praying for Dave Rowe as he undergoes back surgery today. Asking that Your presence be experienced by all involved. Keep Faith calm with the assurance of Your sovereignty. I've felt so yucky all weekend, and I'm asking for Your healing touch as I battle this bug. Comfort Kamala, I pray, as she and her family grieve the loss of her dad. And I pray Your mercy over Ashley, and protection for her sweet innocent children—including the one she's carrying. I know nothing is beyond Your redemption.

January 29th, 2013

Mother's assisted living place will be cleaned out today and tomorrow. It's so sad to me that this woman who always was in control has none now, nor does she appear to want it. I'm thankful for Monica and Kevin who are able to do all the work. It just seems like a rapid digression of her condition. Give me the opportunity to say what I need to say while I can still say it, I ask.

As Mike speaks in California, give him a connection with his audience that will have the effect of communicating the truth and hope. Continue to give Dave Rowe healing and comfort today and give Faith the assurance that You are present and taking care of every detail.

In the midst of Moses' dealing with Pharaoh, You told him to tell Pharaoh, "... *so you may know that there is no one like me in all the earth. For by now I could have stretched out my hand and struck you and your people with a plague that would have wiped you off the earth. But I have raised you up for this very purpose, that I might show you my power and that my name might be proclaimed in all the earth"* (*Exodus 9:14-17*).

Everything You do is purposeful, and it always points people to You. The desire of Your heart is to proclaim Your name in all the earth.

Update #11
January 30ᵗʰ, 2013

My mom got the results back from the gene testing, and they found three genes that malfunctioned and caused the tumor. This test was able to line her up with clinical trials around the country. She matched one in Cincinnati. After getting all the information and reading the side effects of the two medications they wanted to give her, she decided not to go through with the clinical trial. They said there would be no benefit health-wise to doing the trial. Even though the medications were not chemo, they sure did have side effects like it. So she is going to continue seeing the Chinese doctor every week. Her oncologist is still amazed by her increasingly better blood counts. She'll be having a scan next Monday and will get the results next Wednesday. This will be her first scan since mid-November. Please be praying for the results.

february 2013

February 5th, 2013

Getting back to "normal" after a weekend visit with the Barnetts celebrating Anna Kate's third birthday! So much fun, some more snuggle time with Coy.

Yesterday, I had CT scan done—not that I wanted to, but it's the only way to know what's going on inside. Lord, I honestly have no fear of bad news because You are with me. It's just news that others are anxious for. You will fulfill Your purpose for me, and I'm resting in Your sovereignty. As I consider what my mind can even comprehend, I am amazed at Your faithfulness in keeping me in perfect peace. My mind is focused on You, and I just have to trust that those who I love will take advantage of Your promises and know that You will be faithful to them as You have been to me.

Psalm 27:1

The LORD is my light and my salvation—whom shall I fear? The LORD is the stronghold of my life—of whom shall I be afraid?

In other words, because of You, Lord, I have all I need and want. My every need is met. I lack nothing and You keep me in perfect peace. Your presence is my confidence.

Update #12
February 6th, 2013

And now I am at a loss for words. My dad called me a little over two hours ago with the results from my mom's scans. I knew right away the news wasn't going to be good. There are two spots in her lungs that have grown rapidly since her last scan on the 12th of November. One spot in her lower left lobe and one spot in her upper right lobe, each spot measuring about 1 inch x 1 inch. A new cluster of spots have also formed in the upper abdomen, the largest spot measuring roughly a 1/4 inch x 1/4 inch.

The doctor is most concerned about the new appearance of a large mass between her lower left ribs and lungs measuring roughly 3 inches x 2 inches. The doctor seemed to be surprised on how well she is feeling and how well she could take deep breaths without any pain. He is still encouraged that her blood work numbers look really good, meaning that her immune system is running at top form.

So, we keep praying. We keep enjoying the afternoon sunshine. We keep enjoying watching a puppy play. We keep holding onto the Hand that heals. We keep praising.

Each second, each minute, each hour, each day, is precious.

Be light. Be love.
Caleb

February 6th, 2013

Psalm 29:11
The LORD gives strength to his people; the LORD blesses his people with peace.

February 7th, 2013

Yesterday, was the 16th anniversary of my cancer surgery, and the news was not good from the doctor. The cancer has spread, and he is concerned about keeping me pain-free.

What are my thoughts? I honestly had no fear of bad news, but this was overwhelming. I don't want to dwell on the details; I do feel good, and I am confident of Your presence and purpose in all of this. It's just so hard to see Mike, Monica, and the kids have to deal with it. I know they care and are very concerned. Thank You for Your life in me, that I can genuinely experience Your peace and presence. You are amazing, Lord! Your faithfulness to me is completely solid.

Psalm 27:3
Though an army besiege me, my heart will not fear; though war break out against me, even then will I be confident.

Proverbs 8:10-11
Choose my instruction instead of silver, knowledge rather than choice gold, for wisdom is more precious than the rubies, and nothing you desire can compare with her.

Counsel has told us to invest wisely for retirement so that we have enough resources to maintain a reasonable standard of living. Mike has always done such a conscientious job evaluating what we have and what to anticipate as far as needs. Hopefully he's felt my support through the years as I always viewed him as the most wonderful blessing.

We never know for sure what we'll need financially or how long we'll even be on this earth, but what I do know is that You will provide. You always have!

And now as I face life's end, I realize I don't need money, but what I do need I have in amazing abundance. Nothing I have ever desired compares with You and the investment of time spent with You in Your Word. It is paying huge rewards now as I experience Your peace in the face of challenges. You knew what I would need in this season of my life, and although I have "things," what I really need, I have in You.

February 8th, 2013

Psalm 31:14-15a
But I trust in you, O LORD; I say, "You are my God." My times are in your hands.

Indeed they are!

February 9th, 2013

Maggie and Molly arrive today. Looking forward to fun times together. Give them safe and unstressful travel, I pray.

Exodus 29:43
There also I will meet with the Israelites, and the place will be consecrated by my glory.

The place where You meet with Your people is consecrated by Your glory, Lord. I love this truth.

Matthew 26:39
Three times Jesus prayed, *"My father, if it is possible, may this cup be taken from me. Yet not as I will, but as you will."*

If it is possible—all things are possible with You, Lord. But submission to Your perfect will, though tough, is the best place to be. And You give us the freedom to ask and the strength to accept Your answers. What would I do, where would I be, apart from You? I can't imagine, nor would I want to.

Thank You for this day. I rejoice in it!

February 10th, 2013

Mike is off to Houston. Maggie and Molly are here. Should be a fun few days just hanging out and doing girl stuff. I am so thankful for this time!

Psalm 32:7, 10b
You are my hiding place; you will protect me from trouble and surround me with songs of deliverance. . . . The LORD's unfailing love surrounds the man who trusts in him.

I am experiencing Your "surrounding" in new ways as I travel this season. Songs of deliverance whenever I tend to fear have reminded me of Your unfailing love. Wherever I turn, You are there surrounding me with Your faithful protection and love.

February 11th, 2013

Exodus 33:13
If you are pleased with me, teach me your ways so I may know you and continue to find favor with you.

You replied, *"My Presence will go with you, and I will give you rest"* *(Exodus 33:14).*

Your presence gives me rest from the journey, the battle, the struggle—no matter what. Your faithfulness is unfailing. I know this full well.

Thank You for the time of prayer with the elders yesterday—time to approach Your throne in confidence and to testify to Your great faithfulness in my life. You are my great reward.
February 14th, 2013

Molly is on her way home, and I'm reflecting on the wonderful time we had over the last few days. Thank You for Your goodness that afforded us this time.

The shopping was fun and the surprise gift of Katie's boots and the lessons learned. Wow!

Each day is such a gift. I pray we each learn to cherish every one You give us.

Psalm 33:18-19
The eyes of the LORD are on those who fear him, on those whose hope is in his unfailing love, to deliver them from death and keep them alive in famine.

Psalm 34:7-8
The angel of the LORD encamps around those who fear him, and he delivers them. Taste and see that the LORD is good; blessed is the man who takes refuge in him.

Thank You that I know Your eyes are on me for my hope is in You. Your angel is encamped around me and I lack nothing, no good thing.

February 16th, 2013

Praying for the GCC Elders as they retreat to pray and plan. I ask Your guidance and wisdom for them as they seek Your direction. Give them unity, resolve, and strength.

Thank You for Tina and Dave being willing to take care of the dog while we go on our trip. This is such a huge blessing!

Knowing that You are concerned with all the details of my life still amazes me. If You are willing, if it is Your will, You are able to heal or fix anything. I trust You, Lord, to accomplish Your perfect plan even at the cost of my suffering. My discomfort continues, but the joy of the Lord is my strength. You will keep me in perfect peace.

February 17th, 2013

Beth Moore's *The Law of Love* Bible Study

Deuteronomy is a covenant document.

Deuteronomy 1:6-8
The LORD our God said to us at Horeb, "You have stayed long enough at this mountain. Break camp and advance into the hill country. . . . Go in and take possession of the land that the LORD swore he would give to your fathers."

Your desire for me is to not stay camped at a place long term. When the time is right You direct my steps to move forward. Still sometimes I choose to stay longer than You intended. Forgive me Lord. As the days draw near for me to enter Your presence, give me courage to go and take possession of all You have promised. I know my mind can't imagine what this "good land" entails, but I know You well enough to know that being in Your presence will be amazing and there will be no looking back.

Deuteronomy 2:7
The LORD your God has blessed you in all the work of your hands. He has watched over your journey through this vast desert. These forty years the LORD your God has been with you, and you have not lacked anything.

This is my testimony. Having walked with You forty-plus years, I know Your eye and hand has been upon me—Your presence my constant guide—and I have indeed lacked nothing.

December 20th, 2001

You saved me and called me to a holy life because of Your purpose and grace. I may not know much, but through Your revelation to me—Your Word which is equipping me—I know whom I have believed and am persuaded that You are able to keep what I've entrusted to You until that day when You bring me face to face with You and I can rejoice at finishing the race.

August 28th, 2007

As I was meditating just now on fragrance, in the path we take, as related to our legacy as well as our everyday lives, I was brought to 2 Corinthians 2:14 which I painted on the slate that hangs in our bedroom. You always lead in triumph, spreading everywhere I go with a fragrance of what I know of You. Knowledge of You and time spent with You has an effect.

Then I opened my One Year Bible and 2 Corinthians 2:12-17 was today's reading! You continue to amaze me.

March 1st, 2010

What I do know is that I know I am Yours. It takes a lifetime of walking in Your presence as You continue to reveal Yourself. And just when I think I've got it, I realize You are so much more than I can comprehend. You are awesome and I praise You. Thank You for never letting me go and for that amazing "moment" as I walked on Thursday, wandering aimlessly while keeping the hotel in sight. When I came to the end of the road for my return, seeing the bumper sticker on that last car, "Smile, God loves you." You planned that just for me!

The bumper sticker is such a small thing; however, You knew it would be there and it reminded me of Your involvement in the details of my life. My first memory of talking to You from my heart.

February 19th, 2013

In one week, we leave for Rome. I can't believe we're doing this. I do ask for health and strength to make the entire journey for all of us. And that I can go to Rome with Mike as he's always wanted. Thank You for Your goodness to us.

Psalm 37:3-4
Trust in the LORD and do good; dwell in the land and enjoy safe pasture. Delight yourself in the LORD and he will give you the desires of your heart.

Mark 4:18-19
Still others, like seed sown among thorns, hear the word; but the worries of this life, the deceitfulness of wealth and the desires for other things come in and choke the word, making it unfruitful.

I thank You that You have given me a desire for Your Word that has satisfied my heart and enriched my soul beyond anything I could have imagined.

the end precedes the beginning

My mom's last journal entry was on February 19th, 2013. How fitting that in her last entry she talked about how thankful she was that God had given her a desire to read His Word, how it had satisfied her heart and enriched her soul beyond anything she could've imagined. On February 6th, I was ready to come back home after hearing the news from the latest scan. Since the doctor gave approval of going on the cruise, my mom and dad continued along with the plans. I ended up meeting them in Rome on February 27th—the day they arrived. My mom and dad, along with Kylie and Kaitlyn, went straight to St. Peter's Square to see the last public appearance of Pope Benedict. My mom was within five feet of the Pope as he made his last public act by kissing a baby. I met them later in the day at the apartment rental since I flew in later that morning. This was the first time I had seen Mom in six weeks. When I left in January, I thought there was no way the six-month life expectancy the doctor had given her in October was true. She was feeling great. But when I saw her in Rome, I knew right away she wasn't doing well. Even though she was upbeat and had a smile on her face, I could tell the sarcoma was taking over. We enjoyed three days touring Rome and were grateful for dear friends who invested in a personal tour guide and driver for us, making our experience in Rome much more comfortable. I navigated my mom's wheelchair through the cobblestone streets, the Coliseum, the Vatican museum, and finally to the Sistine Chapel. We ended each night with a nightcap of gelato at a place just a few blocks from the apartment.

I left on March 2nd—the day Dad, Mom, Kylie, Kaitlyn, Monica, and her husband Dan boarded the cruise ship. That morning didn't start out so well. My mom was very weak and pale, and I practically had to carry her down the stairs. My dad was ready to call the whole trip off, but my mom thought with all the touring she was just worn out and that as soon as she was on the ship she could rest and would feel better. I left that morning for the airport because I had to return to France to prepare for a football game with my team, which would be taking place the following week. Mom did begin to improve once they were aboard. She even felt good enough to disembark in the port of Rhodes, where she thoroughly enjoyed the markets. My mom celebrated her 64th birthday on-board, and my parents also renewed their vows.

They disembarked the ship on Wednesday, March 13th, and spent one night in Rome before flying home to Atlanta on March 14th. My mom started having trouble breathing halfway through the flight home. Fortunately, there was a pain management doctor, working with cancer patients in Dallas, who was able to sit with her for the remainder of the flight. She emptied three large bottles of oxygen on the flight. Upon arrival in Atlanta, Mom was rushed to the hospital and put in ICU. The decision was made Thursday evening, March 14th, to call the kids because healthcare professionals didn't think my mom would live too much longer. I awoke Friday morning in France and saw the text from my dad. I had about an hour to get ready and then a 45-minute drive to the train station in Grenoble to catch a train to Paris. On the three-hour train ride, I was able to talk to Dad and told him to tell Mom that I loved her. The only thing I wanted was to be able to see her one more time . . . to say "I love you."

Update #13
March 15th, 2013

Two hours ago, I landed in Atlanta. My mom was rushed to the hospital Thursday afternoon after landing from their flight from Rome.

I was able to talk with her for a few minutes—hold her hand and give her a kiss—before she fell asleep again.

In the past month, the sarcoma has grown rapidly. The new spot they found in February between her left ribs and lung has doubled in size, it is now 15 centimeters. This tumor has pretty much shut down her left lung. There are multiple spots on her right lung that have shown up as well. Her breathing is pretty labored, and her heartbeat is between 90 and 100. They are mostly worried about her going into cardiac arrest.

They are going to try to continue to stabilize her and hopefully we can bring her home tomorrow afternoon, or Sunday, where she will be under hospice.

Please be praying.
Caleb

Very early Saturday morning, March 16th, after not being able to sleep that much, I walked over to the hospital to relieve my dad so that he could get a few hours of sleep in a bed. When I entered her room around 5 a.m., my mom was wide awake and looked like a completely different person from the night before. We spent about three hours together eating breakfast and talking. I was having a difficult time accepting that she would not be around to be Grandma Kia to my kids. She told me her memory will live on in my nieces and nephews, and that Kylie and Kaitlyn would be able to tell amazing stories of their grandma to my kids one day. After some tests, she was cleared to go home on hospice that afternoon.

Update #14
March 19th, 2013

Last night, we brought home a big Dairy Queen Oreo ice cream cake, and I asked my mom what she wanted written on the cake. She said, "Celebrating Surprises." On Saturday morning, my dad, sisters, and I had some time all together with Mom before we transferred her home. We have had somewhat of a tradition that every time we get into a pool, we end up having a "pool side confessional," usually pertaining to food addictions or weight problems. Well, this time it was in a hospital room. My dad started out by confessing that the only reason he took his two oldest granddaughters to teen night every evening on the cruise was so that he could go eat a whole pizza at the buffet. Then, my sister Maggie spoke up and confessed that she and her husband, Jeff, were actually married on September 1st, 2011, in South Korea, and not on December 27th, 2011, in North Carolina. Good thing my mom was hooked up to oxygen. We all had a good laugh and have video proof of the confession.

Sunday, my Grandma Rose was dying. Mom was able to talk with her on the phone before she did. Molly,

Maggie, and I went to go see her in Athens. She couldn't see us and could only respond with slight moans. I was able to tell her that I enjoyed spending time with her this past fall. She had a stroke in October, and I spent more time with her in three months than I had in thirty-one years. It was a blessing. I was able to write her several letters and share the gospel with her. We all prayed with her and shared some Bible verses. My aunt told us that Grandma had told the hospice nurse a few days before that she wanted to die before her daughter. My sister Maggie told Grandma that Mom was okay and that we were taking great care of her—that it was okay to go. Grandma passed away five hours later.

Mom has enjoyed being home. The last couple of days have been good. She was able to take a shower and sit in her chair for a while. She sat in her wheelchair for the cake celebration last night. We also took communion together as a family.

I had some alone time with her early Saturday morning and she told me if she had one thing to say to me it would be . . . "Forgive . . . Forgive . . . Forgive . . . Do not judge."

Celebrating Each Day . . .
Caleb

People in the neighborhood opened up their homes so we could all stay close to one another. Mom did really well that first week. On Friday night, March 22nd, we had a little scare. Mom was not feeling well and her heartbeat accelerated. I woke up the next morning with my sister

Maggie telling me that Mom was waiting for me to make her pancakes. She had recovered during the night and was ready for a lumberjack breakfast in the morning! When we all initially came home, we thought that Mom only had days to live. Seeing her like this was a gracious surprise, but unfortunately, my sisters had to get back to work. After talking with the hospice nurse, Molly decided to go back to North Carolina on Monday, March 25th, and Maggie flew back to Colorado on Tuesday the 26th. Katie and her infant son Coy were able to stay, because she was still on maternity leave. With Molly and Maggie, the medical professionals in the family, back at their respective homes, I was left to administer Mom's medications during the night of the 26th.

Update #15
March 27th, 2013

Good Morning,

Last night was the worst night. Pain in her chest, in her heart. Labored breathing. Just keeping her comfortable. Reading her Psalms.

In Eric Metaxas book—*Bonhoeffer: Pastor, Martyr, Prophet, Spy*—Dietrich Bonhoeffer had a good perspective on death:

"Death is mild, death is sweet and gentle; it beckons to us with heavenly power, if only we realize that it is the gateway to our homeland, the tabernacle of joy, the everlasting kingdom of peace." (p. 531)

A prayer I wrote on a sleepless night in France. I wish it would come true.

Make me small / Like those days you knit me / Hem me back in / Behind and before / Fearfully and wonderfully / Make me small / In the comfort of her womb / My warrior's heart will not stay / Pain will draw me / The beast inside her will not be silent / Make me small / Her veins will guide / Being unwound from the beginning / Stable and steadfast / I will make my way to its lair / Make me small / Its hot breath, its evil eyes / Face to face / The sword of my hand / This dragon I will slay / Make me small / It's an easy choice / My darkest valleys / My deepest doubts / It was her prayers / That kept me / Make me small / A time will come / When every beast and dragon / Will be slain / Make me small / She will take a deep breath / There will be no more pain / Make me small / Lord, heal my mom / Or make me small / Heal my mom / Or make me small

Please be praying.
Caleb

On Wednesday, Mom didn't eat her breakfast and she was very incoherent. The hospice nurse came in that afternoon and upped the dose of pain medication. I called Molly, and she started driving back from North Carolina that afternoon. Around 6 p.m. on the evening of the 27th, I was lying next to Mom and my sister Katie came in the room. She started singing, "You Are My Hiding Place." Then with her eyes closed and as loud as she could, Mom started singing along, very slurred but very beautiful.

June 24ᵗʰ, 2010

Not only do You surround the righteous with Your
favor as with a shield, You say in Isaiah 4:5-6: *Then the*
Lᴏʀᴅ will create over all of Mount Zion and over those
who assemble there a cloud of smoke by day and a glow
of flaming fire by night; over all the glory will be a canopy.
It will be a shelter and shade from the heat of the day, and a
refuge and hiding place from the storm and rain.

People talk about "the umbrella" for Your protection,
but I love the canopy word picture. It not only protects
from the effects of the day's heat, providing shelter and
shade, but it is also a refuge and hiding place from the
storm and rain.

You are my hiding place; You fill my heart with songs of
deliverance, whenever I am afraid, I will trust in You.
Under Your canopy of protection, I am safe. I am
surrounded by Your favor like a shield.

Shortly after this song, Mom's last words to me as I lay next to her
were, "I love you, sweetie." We had Maggie on Skype from Colorado.
Molly and her family were on Skype as they were driving to be with
us. Mom's last words were to Maggie. She said, "I love you, Maggie."
Molly arrived around 11 p.m. I started sponging Mom's parched lips
to keep her mouth moist. Everyone else found a spot on the bed.
Around 1 a.m. I left the room and Molly took over with the sponges.
I went to lie down in the living room. Uncertain whether or not I
really slept, I returned to my parents' room around 4 a.m. Molly was
sitting in a chair next to my mom, hunched over, sleeping beside her.
My dad was lying next to his bride and Katie alongside of him. My

mom's breathing was very labored, and it was very difficult to watch her lungs gasp for breath. I took over sponging her lips. Her skin was clammy, and she had cold sweats because of the effort she needed for each breath. I whispered in my mom's ear that I was back. I told her it was okay and that we would be okay. Then I began praying that Jesus would take her—that she wouldn't have to struggle for each breath anymore. At 5:01 a.m. on March 28th, 2013, my mom took her last earthly breath and her first heavenly breath.

My Aunt Monica was cleaning out the room later that day and she noticed a small clock on the dresser that my mom had bought many years before at an antique shop in Paris. The clock had never worked, but my mom liked it as a decoration. The clock read 5:01.

I would like to end this chapter with two letters my mom wrote. The first one to her children, and the second one she wrote to me.

Letter from 2002

After reading Isaiah 61:3, I realize that whatever our source or cause of mourning, only Christ can lift our hearts and heads. Everyone has broken or unfulfilled dreams. Satan wants us to have our dreams destroyed and render us useless. God wants to surpass our dreams. We are never in a place where God is not with us. Trust Him to have a purpose in everything, even though we may feel like we're in a wilderness. God sometimes allows us to be let down and disappointed in life so we will learn to set our hopes more fully in Him.

My prayer for you is that you will have a new understanding and comprehension of who God is and what riches you have in Him that you do not yet realize!

When you're unhappy, that you will look to a change of heart rather than a change of circumstances. I desire for you to have dreams from the realm of knowledge of Him where He can bring you a much more fulfilling reality than you could ever imagine on your own. Take those baby steps of trust and dare to dream the dreams of a child of the King. Delight yourself in Him, and if you don't know what that means or how to do it, ask Him!

November 29th, 2000

Victory, wisdom, growth, and comfort do not happen apart from God's Word! It is a pattern of daily dependence, and I am encouraging you to trust, keep trusting, and don't let your heart become hardened. God can take your honesty—"This sucks God." But He can't speak to you through bitterness and hard-heartedness.

You have so many good and noble qualities, and I am trusting God's sovereignty to use this time in your life to prepare you for something awesome. It literally thrills my soul. Remember that as God's precious child, you have direct access to His throne and can ask Him why and tell Him how you're feeling. He knows! He will lead you, but your heart must be in a condition to be directed. Meditate on Hebrews 4:12-13 and let God's Word penetrate your heart—nothing is hidden from His sight.

My encouragement to you is: Thank God—even though you're not happy with your circumstances—as a way of honoring Him. And then the way will be prepared for you to see His plan unfold.

the beginning

by Katie McCoy Barnett

This journey that we were on is not what we had planned, but it is our journey nonetheless. My mom found out she had cancer on July 7th, 2012, and our lives have never been the same since. My mom was so strong and positive throughout the entire struggle. She completely trusted God and didn't fear this disease or death. I almost wonder if she had regular human emotions, which I know she did, but she didn't dwell on them. She woke up each day, was thankful for that ordained day and lived in the joy of the moment. She didn't think beyond that day, because she didn't want what might be in the future to steal the joy of that day. I could share so many different things concerning my mom, but I want to share one specific thought as you finish this book.

Throughout my life, my mom has always had a fascination with a full moon. I can recall many times when she would call me on the phone asking me if I had looked at the moon. Whenever we were at Camp Fitch or the beach and there was a full moon, it was a very special time. She would always take time to go outside and look at the full moon. There was a full moon over New Years this past year when my family was at the beach together, and we all spent time on the deck overlooking the ocean and enjoying the beauty of that full moon.

That was such a precious time to me. I wondered that night if we would ever be looking at a full moon together as a family again. She started this with her grandchildren as well—telling them she loved them to the moon and back, buying story books about the moon, and getting them to look at it. I remember, in August 2012, when I was at her house visiting, there was a blue moon—which means it is the second full moon in one month. We walked outside and looked at it that evening, knowing that the next blue moon wouldn't be until August 2013. I prayed that I would get to see the next blue moon with my mom, but God had other plans. When I found out that there was going to be a full moon on March 27th, 2013, I had a feeling that she would leave us then.

My mom is a very reflective person. Many times we wondered what she was thinking, but what we didn't fully realize was that she was very outspoken—just in the written word. She started journaling about fifteen years ago and was faithful with it. We have 23 full journals up in her "happy room." They're full of her beautiful handwriting—words reflecting on what God was teaching her, prayers for her children and family, and words of wisdom. On the night she was dying, Caleb was reading her latest journal, which she started at the beginning of her cancer diagnosis. In that journal, she wrote down why she has such a fascination with the full moon.

She says, "The full moon—I have always been awed by it and hopefully have transferred that to my children and grandchildren. I remember the full moon rising over the Atlantic at Hilton Head on a June evening, absolutely breathtaking, and I've grown to appreciate the wonder of God's creation so much that I put the dates of the yearly full moons on my calendar." She continues on to quote Ann Voskamp, the author of *One Thousand Gifts,* who helps put words to her fascination with the full moon: "Joy that fills me under a full moon is the joy that always fills God. God sees it all. This is His endless experience because He is who He is. My moon wonder is but a glimpse, a foretaste of what God always sees, experiences. Joy is God's life." (p. 117) My mom finishes with, "Joy fills me under a full moon too, reminding me of God's faithfulness and the wonder of His dependability, an obvious sign of His trustworthiness."

Psalm 19 says, *"The heavens declare the glory of God; the skies proclaim the work of his hands. Day after day they pour forth speech; night after night they display knowledge. There is no speech or language where their voice is not heard. Their voice goes out into all the earth, their words to the ends of the world. In the heavens he has pitched a tent for the sun, which is like a bridegroom coming forth from his pavilion, like a champion rejoicing to run his course. It rises at one end of the heavens and makes its circuit to the other; nothing is hidden from its heat."*

The moon is full when its face is completely turned towards the sun and thus fully reflects the sun. The moon has no shine on its own. It is merely reflecting the light of the sun. I liken that to my mother. She was a true full moon with her face towards the Son, her Savior, completely reflecting His characteristics of love, joy, peace, patience, kindness, goodness, faithfulness, and self-control. She truly radiated the light of Christ and never wavered from this even in the face of a terminal illness.

So, after all these years, here is my answer: My mom loved full moons because they were a sign of God's faithfulness and dependability in her life, and she wanted that transferred to her children and grandchildren. What a way to really hammer down a point Mom, when you leave this Earth on a full moon. I think we get it. You want us to know that God is faithful, dependable, and trustworthy. You want us to know we can believe His Word and that He is who He says He is. I love that I'll have that constant reminder in the night sky of God's faithfulness and of you.

An interesting revelation came through a letter to my mom's sister, Monica, after a friend learned about Mom's passing. In the letter, her friend states, "I have been learning Hebrew over the last year as a way of getting to understand the culture and language that our Redeemer chose to live and communicate through. When you mentioned Kia's fascination with the moon and how especially bright it was the night she died, I couldn't help but connect that to how Scripture uses the moon as a picture of the Bride. The moon at its fullest speaks in the natural world of the Bride fully walking in the light of her bridegroom, completely bathed by the brilliance of His purity as she turns completely away from darkness and every sin that so easily besets her. Our Savior died on a full moon; God gave us this heavenly sign to mark the timing of the Passover. It couldn't be more profound that your sister went into His presence clinging to nothing but the beautiful spotless illuminated covering He provided for her during the time of a full moon."

One of my mom's greatest desires was to leave behind a legacy. She has left more than that with the blessing of her handwritten journal entries. Her thoughts, prayers, and defining moments that I know my family will treasure in the days and years to come. Thank you, Mom, for your dedication to the Lord and to journaling. You will continue to bless so many people through your words.

And to all of you who have read this book, I can only imagine what my mom would say to you now. She would tell you to, "Trust God, know that He is completely sovereign, quit worrying, and live for joy each day. Don't sweat the small stuff. Forgive, forgive, forgive; nothing is worth holding on to."

And Mom, you've made such an impact and will continue to do so through your words. I am so glad I have them. I know in my heart that March 28th, 2013, at 5:01 a.m. was not the end of your life, it was truly the beginning. You are more alive today than you ever were. You are with our Savior, and I can only imagine what you are experiencing! We can't wait to be reunited again someday soon. Until then, we say, "See you later." I can't wait to join the party with you someday. We love you so much.

acknowledgements

Gratitude. This book couldn't have happened without so many of you helping me along the way. To you, I say thank you.

Chris Reis, you went down a similar road, and when you shared what you have learned, you helped me immensely. Keep living for more.

Elizabeth Walters, your willingness to take on the project of typing out all the selected journal entries and then being able to understand all my sticky notes still amazes me. Keep dancing.

Sarah Collins, you perfectly captured what was in my head for the book cover. Keep imagining. Keep creating.

Katy Kornegay, your encouragement and lending ear was greatly appreciated through this entire process. Especially, at the end. I couldn't have done it without you.

Steven Paschall—the master of photo editing and beyond that—your depth of insight and input amaze me. You are the brother I never had. Under the mercy.

Laurin Greco, you took on the job of editing in the midst of planning a wedding and getting married. I am forever grateful. Know too that my mom loved you like you were her fourth daughter. A special thank you to John as well. I know you spent many hours next to Laurin as she worked through these journals. It was perfect timing.

Monica, your stories and background information helped me compile the story and give it so much more depth. Thank you for encouraging my mom to get back out on the ice.

Molly, Maggie, Katie—I wouldn't be who I am if it wasn't for you guys. You are aliens as well, and I can't wait for the party in the land for which we were made. I love you—all three of you—equally, the same.

Dad, without the support and food, I couldn't have finished this book. Keep fighting the good fight, keep running the race, keep the faith. Finish strong. I love you.

And finally, I wrote this book to honor my mom and to honor my God, My Savior. There will be tears of joy when I will see you both.

notes

All Bibles verses from:

All scripture quotations, unless otherwise indicated, are taken from the Holy Bible, New International Version®, NIV®. Copyright © 1973, 1978, 1984 by Biblica, Inc.™ Used by permission of Zondervan. All rights reserved worldwide. www.zondervan.com The "NIV" and "New International Version" are trademarks registered in the United States Patent and Trademark Office by Biblica, Inc.™

Other sources:

Ann Voskamp, *One Thousand Gifts: A dare to live fully right where you are* (Zondervan); 2010, page 117

Eric Metaxas, *Bonhoeffer: Pastor, Martyr, Prophet, Spy* (Thomas Nelson Inc.); 2010, page 531

Dietriech Bonhoeffer, *Life Together: A discussion of Christian fellowship* (Harper and Row Publishers, Inc.); 1954, page 43

Sheldon Vanauken, *A Severe Mercy* (Harper San Francisco—A division of Harper Collins Publishers); 1977, page 119, 121, 125, 226, 227, 228

about the author

Caleb Patrick McCoy was born on April 1st, 1981, in Erie, Pennsylvania, and in 1989 his family moved to Atlanta, Georgia. Growing up he enjoyed playing sports and excelled in football and basketball. Caleb spent the summer of 2003 working at the youth camp *Le Camp des Cimes* in the French Alps. He returned each summer during college, and after receiving his degree in outdoor leadership from Western State Colorado University in 2006, Caleb moved to France. Following a year of studying the French language, he began working full time at *Le Camp des Cimes*. Around the same time, he also started playing American football for a regional club team and has been coaching and playing since 2007. Leading theater workshops for the French youth gave Caleb a passion for acting, and since 2010 he has spent each fall in the Atlanta area working in television and film.

Please visit the website:

www.angelonice.com

You can view my mom's "Amazing Grace" performance and more photos, as well as purchase more books.
Please leave a comment about the book, share a story—we would love to hear from you.

Please visit the Mike McCoy Ministries website:

www.mccoy77.com

Net proceeds of this book will go to MMM, Inc.

Mercy Ministries

www.mercyministries.org

Ara Parseghian Medical Research Foundation

www.parseghian.org

Invite Mike McCoy and or Caleb McCoy to Speak at Your Event

contact: Kelly@FieldofPlayMarketing.com

or call 412-680-3222

or fill out a request form at:

www.fieldofplaymarketing.com/athletic-clients/book-mike-mc-coyor-caleb-mccoy-for-your-event.com